JUNIOR DRUG AWARENESS

Over-the-Counter Drugs

JUNIOR DRUG AWARENESS

JUNIOR DRUG AWARENESS

Over-the-Counter Drugs

Johanna Knowles

CHELSEA HOUSE
PUBLISHERS
An imprint of Infobase Publishing

Junior Drug Awareness: Over-the-Counter Drugs
Copyright © 2008 by Infobase Publishing

Chelsea House
An imprint of Infobase Publishing
132 West 31st Street
New York NY 10001

Library of Congress Cataloging-in-Publication Data

Knowles, Johanna.
  Over-the-counter drugs / Johanna Knowles.
    p. cm. — (Junior drug awareness)
  Includes bibliographical references and index.
  ISBN 978-0-7910-9759-5 (hardcover)
  1. Drugs, Nonprescription—Juvenile literature. 2. Drug abuse—Juvenile literature.
I. Title. II. Series.

  RM671.A1K66 2008
  615'.1—dc22   2007043665

Chelsea House books are available at special discounts when purchased in bulk quantities for businesses, associations, institutions, or sales promotions. Please call our Special Sales Department in New York at (212) 967-8800 or (800) 322-8755.

You can find Chelsea House on the World Wide Web
at http://www.chelseahouse.com

Text design by Erik Lindstrom
Cover design by Jooyoung An

Printed in the United States

Bang NMSG 10 9 8 7 6 5 4 3 2 1

This book is printed on acid-free paper.

All links and web addresses were checked and verified to be correct at the time of publication. Because of the dynamic nature of the web, some addresses and links may have changed since publication and may no longer be valid.

CONTENTS

Battling a Pandemic: A History of Drugs in the United States

When Johnny came marching home again after the Civil War, he probably wasn't marching in a very straight line. This is because Johnny, like 400,000 of his fellow drug-addled soldiers, was addicted to morphine. With the advent of morphine and the invention of the hypodermic needle, drug addiction became a prominent problem during the nineteenth century. It was the first time such widespread drug dependence was documented in history.

Things didn't get much better in the later decades of the nineteenth century. Cocaine and opiates were used as over-the-counter "medicines." Of course, the most famous was Coca-Cola, which actually did contain cocaine in its early days.

After the turn of the twentieth century, drug abuse was spiraling out of control, and the United States government stepped in with the first regulatory controls. In 1906, the Pure Food and Drug Act became a law. It required the labeling of product ingredients. Next came the Harrison Narcotics Tax Act of 1914, which outlawed illegal importation or distribution of cocaine and opiates. During this time, neither the medical community nor the general population was aware of the principles of addiction.

After the passage of the Harrison Act, drug addiction was not a major issue in the United States until the 1960s, when drug abuse became a much bigger social problem. During this time, the federal government's drug enforcement agencies were found to be ineffective. Organizations often worked against one another, causing counterproductive effects. By 1973, things had gotten so bad that President Richard Nixon, by executive order, created the Drug Enforcement Administration (DEA), which became the lead agency in all federal narcotics investigations. It continues in that role to this day. The effectiveness of enforcement and the so-called "Drug War" are open to debate. Cocaine use has been reduced by 75% since its peak in 1985. However, its replacement might be methamphetamine (speed, crank, crystal), which is arguably more dangerous and is now plaguing the country. Also, illicit drugs tend to be cyclical, with various drugs, such as LSD, appearing, disappearing, and then reappearing again. It is probably closest to the truth to say that a war on drugs can never be won, just managed.

Fighting drugs involves a three-pronged battle. Enforcement is one prong. Education and prevention is the second. Treatment is the third.

Although pandemics of drug abuse have been with us for more than 150 years, education and prevention were not seriously considered until the 1970s. In 1982, former First Lady Betty Ford made drug treatment socially acceptable with the opening of the Betty Ford Center. This followed her own battle with addiction. Other treatment centers—including Hazelden, Fair Oaks, and Smithers (now called the Addiction Institute of New York)—added to the growing number of clinics, and soon detox facilities were in almost every city. The cost of a single day in one of these facilities is often more than $1,000, and the effectiveness of treatment centers is often debated. To this day, there is little regulation over who can practice counseling.

It soon became apparent that the most effective way to deal with the drug problem was prevention by education. By some estimates, the overall cost of drug abuse to society exceeds $250 billion per year; preventive education is certainly the most cost-effective way to deal with the problem. Drug education can save people from misery, pain, and ultimately even jail time or death. In the early 1980s, First Lady Nancy Reagan started the "Just Say No" program. Although many scoffed at the program, its promotion of total abstinence from drugs has been effective with many adolescents. In the late 1980s, drug education was not science based, and people essentially were throwing mud at the wall to see what would stick. Motivations of all types spawned hundreds, if not thousands, of drug-education programs. Promoters of some programs used whatever political clout they could muster to get on various government agencies' lists of most effective programs. The bottom line, however, is that prevention is very difficult to quantify. It's nearly impossible to prove that drug use would have occurred if it were not prevented from happening.

In 1983, the Los Angeles Unified School District, in conjunction with the Los Angeles Police Department, started what was considered at that time to be the gold standard of school-based drug education programs. The program was called Drug Abuse Resistance Education, otherwise known as D.A.R.E. The program called for specially trained police officers to deliver drug-education programs in schools. This was an era in which community-oriented policing was all the rage. The logic was that kids would give street credibility to a police officer who spoke to them about drugs. The popularity of the program was unprecedented. It spread all across the country and around the world. Ultimately, 80% of American school districts would utilize the program. Parents, police officers, and kids all loved it. Unexpectedly, a special bond was formed between the kids who took the program and the police officers who ran it. Even in adulthood, many kids remember the name of their D.A.R.E. officer.

By 1991, national drug use had been halved. In any other medical-oriented field, this figure would be astonishing. The number of people in the United States using drugs went from about 25 million in the early 1980s to 11 million in 1991. All three prongs of the battle against drugs vied for government dollars, with each prong claiming credit for the reduction in drug use. There is no doubt that each contributed to the decline in drug use, but most people agreed that preventing drug abuse before it started had proved to be the most effective strategy. The National Institute on Drug Abuse (NIDA), which was established in 1974, defines its mandate in this way: "NIDA's mission is to lead the Nation in bringing the power of science to bear on drug abuse and addiction." NIDA leaders were the experts in prevention and treatment, and they had enormous resources. In

1986, the nonprofit Partnership for a Drug-Free America was founded. The organization defined its mission as, "Putting to use all major media outlets, including TV, radio, print advertisements and the Internet, along with the pro bono work of the country's best advertising agencies." The Partnership for a Drug-Free America is responsible for the popular campaign that compared "your brain on drugs" to fried eggs.

The American drug problem was front-page news for years up until 1990–1991. Then the Gulf War took over the news, and drugs never again regained the headlines. Most likely, this lack of media coverage has led to some peaks and valleys in the number of people using drugs, but there has not been a return to anything near the high percentage of use recorded in 1985. According to the University of Michigan's 2006 Monitoring the Future study, which measured adolescent drug use, there were 840,000 fewer American kids using drugs in 2006 than in 2001. This represents a 23% reduction in drug use. With the exception of prescription drugs, drug use continues to decline.

In 2000, the Robert Wood Johnson Foundation recognized that the D.A.R.E. Program, with its tens of thousands of trained police officers, had the top state-of-the-art delivery system of drug education in the world. The foundation dedicated $15 million to develop a cutting-edge prevention curriculum to be delivered by D.A.R.E. The new D.A.R.E. program incorporates the latest in prevention and education, including high-tech, interactive, and decision-model-based approaches. D.A.R.E. officers are trained as "coaches" who support kids as they practice research-based refusal strategies in high-stakes peer-pressure environments. Through stunning magnetic resonance imaging (MRI) images, students get to see tangible proof of how various substances diminish brain activity.

Will this program be the solution to the drug problem in the United States? By itself, probably not. It is simply an integral part of a larger equation that everyone involved hopes will prevent kids from ever starting to use drugs. The equation also requires guidance in the home, without which no program can be effective.

Ronald J. Brogan
Regional Director
D.A.R.E America

1

Over the Counter and Into Whose Hands?

The doors to the emergency room burst open. Emergency technicians rush a stretcher into the room. A teenager is unconscious. The doctors and nurses hurry to hook him up to life support.

Later, his friends tell the doctors that he had chugged down an entire bottle of cough medicine and had started to **hallucinate**. Then he passed out and they couldn't get him to wake up. At first they were afraid to call for help because they didn't want to get into trouble. But when they tried everything and couldn't wake him up, they finally called 911. Their call probably saved his life.

Lucky for this teenager, he was okay after a few days. But unfortunately, this scene has become all too familiar in emergency rooms across the country. In the past

10 years, the number of emergency calls to a single California poison control center have increased by 10 times. Many healthcare workers and other concerned citizens have begun to realize that over-the-counter drug abuse is a serious problem across the country.

WHAT ARE OTC DRUGS?

If you open the average person's medicine cabinet, you will probably find a variety of medications, such as pain relievers, cough medicines, allergy medications, stomach pain medications, and so on. Most of these types of medicines can be bought at your local drugstore or pharmacy without a **prescription**—a written note from a doctor. Many convenience stores, grocery stores, and airports sell these drugs too. Some rest areas on the highway even sell these medicines in vending machines. Plus, you can buy them on the Internet. These drugs are called over-the-counter medications, or OTC drugs. "Over-the-counter" means that a person doesn't need a prescription to buy them.

Today in the United States, there are more than 80 categories of OTC drugs. Drugs are put into categories according to what they are meant to treat. For example, there are drugs to treat cold-related symptoms, drugs to treat acne, drugs to help people lose weight, drugs to help people quit smoking, and on and on.

OTC drugs come in many forms. Some are liquid, some are pills, and some are gums, lotions, sprays, or patches. OTC drugs are considered very convenient because they treat common symptoms and people do not have to visit their doctor in order to buy them.

Why are some drugs available over the counter and some not? The United States Food and Drug Administration (FDA) is an organization that determines whether or not a drug is safe, and whether it can be sold without

Because over-the-counter medications are commonly used and accessible, many people believe they are safe. When these medicines are not used according to their directions, however, the results can be harmful.

a prescription. Each year the organization tests thousands of drugs before they are made available to the public. They also make sure that all of these drugs are properly **manufactured** and **distributed**. In addition to this, the FDA requires that all OTC drugs have a **drug facts label**. This label tells what the medicine is and what the medicine is supposed to treat. OTC medications also must list the *active* ingredients—those ingredients that actually treat the problem—and include instructions for proper doses based on age and weight. OTC medications also must have warnings about the safety of taking the medicine if you are taking any other medicines, if you are pregnant, or if you are below a certain age.

But despite efforts to keep OTC drugs safe, they still pose a risk, especially to young people. That's because for as long as there have been OTC drugs, there have been people who have misused them. But recently, the numbers of people abusing these drugs has gone up, causing drug companies, the FDA, sellers of OTC drugs,

SAFE ENOUGH FOR OUR SIDE OF THE COUNTER?

The FDA has strict and specific guidelines for approving drugs to be sold over the counter. These general rules always apply:

- The benefits of the drug must outweigh the risks of the drug.
- The risk that people will misuse or abuse the drug must be considered low.
- People who buy the drug must be able to use it for a condition they are certain they have, without needing to ask a doctor about it. In other words, the condition the drug treats needs to be one that is easy to diagnose yourself, such as a headache, fever, runny nose, or sore muscles.
- All of a drug's known safety information (such as possible side effects and ingredients) must be provided on the label.
- The medication should be safe to take without the supervision of a doctor or other healthcare professional who is qualified to write prescriptions.

and people in the community to become increasingly concerned.

USE VS. ABUSE

Sometimes people take more than the recommended dose of an OTC drug. They may think that taking a larger dose will make them feel better faster. And sometimes people take OTC drugs even when they don't have any of the symptoms that the drug is supposed to treat. They may do this because they like the way the drug makes them feel. In some cases, people take a *lot* more than the recommended dose in order to enhance the drug's side effects, such as feeling light-headed, dizzy, or out of control. Taking more than the recommended dose of an OTC medicine is drug abuse—the same thing as smoking **marijuana** or doing cocaine. It may seem harmless, but in reality, it can be life threatening.

The most commonly abused OTC drugs are ones that have a powerful chemical ingredient called dextromethorphan, or **DXM**. DXM is considered a safe ingredient, but when taken in very high doses, it can produce a "high" feeling. It can also have serious—and dangerous—side effects.

Out of all the OTC drugs that are available in the United States, more than 100 of them contain DXM. Drugs that have DXM come in liquid or tablets. The tablets often pose the greatest danger because, for most people, it's a lot easier to swallow pills than it is to take strong-tasting liquid medicine. The pill forms also have stronger amounts of DXM. This means that people who take it in pill form are increasing their risk of overdose even more.

DXM medicines are not the only OTC drugs that young people abuse. Many also abuse diet pills, sleeping pills, pills for motion sickness, and many others.

OTC DOES NOT ALWAYS MEAN SAFE

A lot of people think that if a medicine is sold over the counter, it's safe. But the people in charge of creating and regulating drugs assume that customers will take the recommended doses listed on the packaging and on the label. These products are only considered safe when used properly. A product that many people use to safely help relieve symptoms of a common cold can quickly become a serious danger when in the hands of someone who plans to take far more than the recommended dose. The dangers are especially high for young people because they often weigh less than the average adult, and a smaller person will experience an even stronger effect from these drugs.

In addition to the short-term health effects of abusing OTC drugs, these medications have many long-term effects. These include psychological **addiction**, and also serious physical problems that can be life threatening, such as brain damage and damage to the liver and other internal organs.

WHO ABUSES OTC DRUGS?

Many people believe the reason young people abuse OTC drugs is because they are legal, inexpensive, and easier to get than illegal drugs such as marijuana. Getting OTC drugs is often as easy as opening the medicine cabinet in their own homes. Many young people also say they choose OTC drugs over **illicit** drugs because they think they are safer. They might get in trouble with their parents if they get caught abusing them, but they don't risk going to jail.

According to The Partnership for a Drug-Free America, studies have shown that 1 out of 10 teens in the United States (more than 2 million people) have abused

(continues on page 20)

OTC DRUG ADDICTION: A DOWNWARD AND DEADLY SPIRAL

Perhaps one of the most dangerous things about assuming that OTC drugs are safe is that people think they can take any amount, for as long as they want—even though the warning labels often say not to take the drug for more than a certain number of days. The truth is, for many young people, taking even twice the recommended dose can cause a very bad reaction. Thus, the dangers of taking even larger quantities over a long period of time are even more troubling. Yet, this is what happens when people become addicted to OTC and other drugs.

Many people try OTC drugs for fun when they are with friends. On Web sites, people talk about how "cool" it is, or they share tips about which drugs have the "best" effects. A young person might try using an OTC drug for fun with friends, but pretty soon they're pushing each other to take bigger and bigger doses for more and more powerful effects. Frequent use of these drugs can then lead to addiction, along with all of the other effects on health. In fact, it's a downward spiral from first use to more frequent use to addiction. And the more a person abuses the drugs, the more devastating the long-term effects are.

In addition to the health risks that come with addiction, there are social and emotional costs. Being addicted to something can affect every aspect of life, from how well you sleep, what you eat, how you do in school, how you interact with your friends and family members, and the choices you make. And although many OTC drugs are

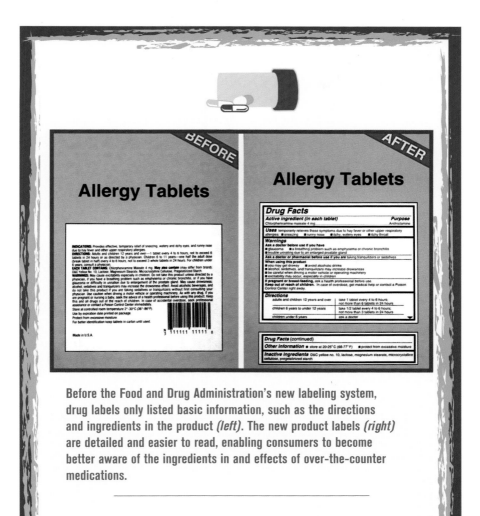

Before the Food and Drug Administration's new labeling system, drug labels only listed basic information, such as the directions and ingredients in the product *(left)*. The new product labels *(right)* are detailed and easier to read, enabling consumers to become better aware of the ingredients in and effects of over-the-counter medications.

fairly affordable, heavy use adds up. Many people who become addicted to OTC drugs end up stealing from their parents, their friends' medicine cabinets, or directly from stores.

For many OTC drug addicts, the downward spiral happens quickly. It can also lead to the abuse of prescription drugs and illegal drugs.

(continued from page 17)

cough medicine. In addition, many drug treatment centers have been reporting a shocking new trend in the rise of OTC drug abuse. One treatment center in the Midwest reported that 80% of their patients had abused OTC drugs.

Another study—reported in the journal *Archives of Pediatrics and Adolescent Medicine*—looked at drug use by teens living in California. It showed that the overall percentage of teens using illegal drugs was down slightly in 2006 (compared to survey results from the 1990s), but that use of OTC drugs was increasing. The report noted that three-fourths of the people who said they had abused OTC drugs were between the ages of 9 and 17. This same study showed that between 1999 and 2004, the number of calls received at the California Poison Control System regarding OTC drug abuse increased by 50% each year. National poison control centers also reported increases in youth OTC drug abuse.

In this same California study, 3 out of 5 parents said that they had talked with their children about the risks of using illegal drugs. But only one-third of those parents said that they had talked with their children about the risks of using legal drugs, such as prescription and non-prescription medicines. Perhaps not surprisingly, many parents talk with their children about abusing alcohol and illegal drugs, but not OTC drugs. The biggest reason for this is that many parents have no idea teens are turning to OTC drugs to get high. Awareness of the problem is starting to catch on, though, and many people are trying to make an effort to limit teen access to these drugs.

PUTTING THE BRAKES ON OTC DRUG ABUSE

Because of the growing OTC drug abuse trend, the Drug Enforcement Administration (DEA) now classifies DXM

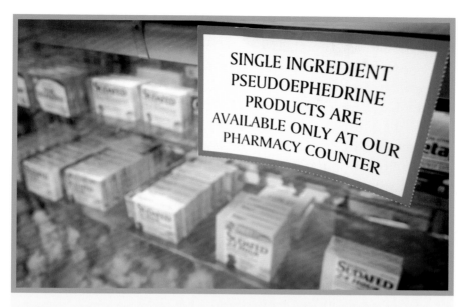

SINGLE INGREDIENT PSEUDOEPHEDRINE PRODUCTS ARE AVAILABLE ONLY AT OUR PHARMACY COUNTER

Recent spikes in over-the-counter drug abuse have led many stores and pharmacies to restrict the sale of medications. Some states have drafted laws to limit or track the sale of pseudoephedrine, a common ingredient in basic allergy medications. Like many products with DXM, psuedoephedrine is abused, but it is more commonly used to manufacture homemade methamphetamines.

as a "drug of concern." DXM has this label because of the dangers it poses when misused. Even though the DEA acknowledges the dangers, there are still no laws or legal restrictions for buying products that contain DXM.

Many drug manufacturers have expressed concerns about the misuse of their products, but they have resisted efforts that others have made to restrict access to the drugs. The reason for this may be that restricting how they sell their products would possibly result in less money made in sales. However, many stores that sell these drugs have begun to try to prevent young people from buying them. Stores sometimes keep certain products behind the counter, which requires customers to request them. The idea behind this is that young people will be less likely to try to buy OTC drugs if they have to ask for them. Other stores have tried to limit the amount of these drugs that individuals can buy over a certain time period. And still other stores have decided not to sell any products that contain DXM to anyone under the age of 18.

Despite all of these efforts, there is a long way to go in keeping OTC drugs away from the people who want to abuse them. Many people believe that the best way to prevent OTC drug abuse and its devastating effects is to educate students and parents about these drugs and the dangers of abusing them.

2

A Closer Look at DXM

Here are just a few true feelings and stories related to DXM:

"I tried taking cough medicine once. It made me feel really strange, like I couldn't control my arms and legs."

"My friends dared me to chug a bottle of cold medicine, so I did it. Everyone told me I acted really funny so I did it again the next day. After a while, I felt like I had to have it. I couldn't stop."

"My best friend told me that taking the cold pills helped her escape her problems. I didn't know she was taking them every day. When she didn't show up for school one morning, I tried to call her. She never answered. I found out later she'd been rushed to the hospital from an overdose. When her mom found out I knew what she'd been up to and never said anything, she was really mad at me."

DXM: NOT ALWAYS "SAFE AND EFFECTIVE"

DXM has been proven safe and effective in treating certain illness symptoms. It has also been proven that it isn't physically addictive. Yet, abusing drugs with DXM is far from safe. Stories like the previous quotes have been told by hundreds of young people across the country. They thought OTC drugs were safe. They thought they were fun. They didn't think abusing OTC drugs was serious.

It's true that studies on DXM and addiction have shown that the drug does not create a physical addiction. This means that if a person uses the drug, his or her body does not react by wanting more, as is the case with other addictive drugs. Studies also show that with continued use, DXM does not lose its effectiveness. This means that if a person uses DXM, he or she doesn't have to take more and more to continue to get the desired effects. Also, people do not have **withdrawal** symptoms if they stop using DXM, as they would with many other drugs.

However, people who abuse DXM may develop a psychological dependence on the effects of the drug. This means that although they don't physically crave the drug, in their minds, they still want to use it. Also, people who experience the effects of taking large doses of DXM often want to see if they can get even higher, or experience even more extreme results. So although DXM isn't considered physically addictive, and it has been proven safe when taken in the *recommended* amounts, it doesn't mean the drug can't be abused—and be deadly.

DXM is a synthetic drug, meaning that it is produced by a chemical process, rather than naturally occurring in, for example, a plant. In 1954 the Food and Drug Administration approved DXM for use as a cough medicine. It is classified as a non-narcotic drug, which means that it is not addictive (people who use it will not develop a physical dependence on it). The chemical works by changing the messages about coughing that are sent to the brain. Instead of coughing the moment the brain senses the need to cough, the brain doesn't notice the need as quickly as it would without medicine.

DXM'S BRIEF HISTORY

DXM's history from approval by the U.S. Food and Drug Administration (FDA) to the present day is a study in how drugs that are meant to help can be regulated as concerns about their abuse grow.

1954   FDA approves DXM for use as a cough medicine.

1970s   FDA replaces codeine with DXM as an OTC cough medicine.

1973   Romilar is taken off the market.

1990s   Reports of DXM abuse are on the rise.

1993   FDA issues an alert, warning parents of DXM abuse.

2005   FDA releases a paper outlining concerns about growing abuse of DXM.

2006   Congressmen Fred Upton and Rick Larsen introduce legislation in the U.S. House of Representatives to restrict the sale of DXM to teenagers.

2007   Senator Joseph R. Biden, Jr., introduces a resolution to designate August as National Medicine Abuse Awareness Month.

When it was first developed, **dextromethorphan** (DXM) was considered safer than the drug **codeine**, and in the 1970s, the FDA replaced codeine with DXM as an over-the-counter cough medicine. Codeine was a strong ingredient used to treat similar symptoms, but it was also highly addictive. DXM was thought to be non-addictive and it had very few, if any, side effects. Since the 1970s, the number of products containing DXM has continued to rise. It is found in many cough syrups, tablets, and gel caps.

Even before DXM replaced codeine, some people were already finding ways to abuse the drug. DXM was in a cough medicine called Romilar. When taken in large amounts, the effects created a high feeling. The drug became so widely abused, it was eventually considered unsafe for OTC use. Beginning in 1973, it was no longer sold.

Still, DXM continued to be used in many OTC drugs. It remained a safe alternative to codeine, and became an active ingredient in more than a hundred over-the-counter cough and cold medications. But with the rise of DXM-containing products came a rise in DXM abuse. By the 1990s, reports of DXM abuse were spreading. In 1993, the FDA issued an alert, warning parents and schools about the increase in DXM abuse among young people. This happened after a series of people overdosed in and around Detroit, Michigan.

Then, on May 20, 2005, the FDA released a paper that outlined its concerns about the growing abuse of DXM. Even though the FDA still considered the drug safe and effective when used as recommended, the agency was concerned about reported deaths due to overdose.

In 2006, representatives Fred Upton from Michigan and Rick Larsen from Washington led the U.S. House of Representatives to pass the Dextromethorphan Distribution Act of 2006. The legislation aimed to restrict the

In an effort to increase awareness about the dangers of medicine abuse, Senator Joseph Biden *(above)* and Congress have declared August as "National Medicine Abuse Awareness Month." Organizations including the Consumer Healthcare Products Association and the Partnership for a Drug-Free America have special drug awareness campaigns that will run in various media each August in an effort to educate people about the dangers of misusing medicine.

sale of raw, unfinished DXM to teenagers. But the bill failed to reach the Senate prior to adjournment.

On June 7, 2007, Senator Joseph R. Biden, Jr., introduced a resolution that proclaimed August National Medicine Abuse Awareness Month. During this month, students and parents all across the United States learned about the dangers of OTC drug abuse. One organization, the Consumer Healthcare Products Association, helped states sponsor town meetings to discuss the growing

(continues on page 30)

DRUG FACTS: CHECK THE LABEL

The Food and Drug Administration requires that all OTC drugs have a drug facts section on the label. The label has several different sections:

ACTIVE INGREDIENT

The first item on the label is the active ingredient section. This lists the chemical contained in the medicine, and how many milligrams of it can be found in the package. It also gives the purpose of the drug. For example, a label might say *antihistamine* if it is used to treat allergies.

USES

This section lists all the symptoms the drug may be used to treat. This section may also be labeled *Indications*. The symptoms listed are ones that the FDA has approved the drug to treat. This means the drug has been tested to treat these symptoms and that it has been proven safe and effective by the FDA.

WARNINGS

This section is broken into different parts, such as allergy alerts, side effects to watch for, and whether you should talk to a doctor before taking the drug. For example, the label may tell you to ask a doctor before taking the drug if you have certain health conditions or specific symptoms. The warning section also tells you about possible side effects, such as drowsiness or dizziness. It may say to avoid driving if you take the drug. It may say not to take the drug with alcohol or certain medications. The label

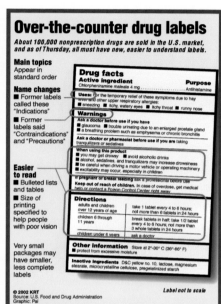

Over-the-counter drug labels

About 100,000 nonprescription drugs are sold in the U.S. market, and as of Thursday, all must have new, easier to understand labels.

Main topics
Appear in standard order

Name changes
■ Former labels called these "Indications"

■ Former labels said "Contraindications" and "Precautions"

Easier to read
■ Bulleted lists and tables
■ Size of printing specified to help people with poor vision

Very small packages may have smaller, less complete labels

Drug facts

Active ingredient   **Purpose**
Chlorpheniramine maleate 4 mg .... Antihistamine

Uses: For the temporary relief of these symptoms due to hay fever and other upper respiratory allergies:
■ sneezing ■ itchy, watery eyes ■ itchy throat ■ runny nose

Warnings
Ask a doctor before use if you have
■ glaucoma ■ trouble urinating due to an enlarged prostate gland
■ a breathing problem such as emphysema or chronic bronchitis

Ask a doctor or pharmacist before use if you are taking tranquilizers or sedatives

When using this product
■ you may get drowsy ■ avoid alcoholic drinks
■ alcohol, sedatives, and tranquilizers may increase drowsiness
■ be careful when driving a motor vehicle or operating machinery
■ excitability may occur, especially in children

If pregnant or breast-feeding ask a professional before use
Keep out of reach of children. In case of overdose, get medical help or contact a Poison Control Center right away.

Directions

adults and children over 12 years of age	take 1 tablet every 4 to 6 hours; not more than 6 tablets in 24 hours
children 6 through 11 years	break tablets in half; take 1/2 tablet every 4 to 6 hours; not more than 3 whole tablets in 24 hours
children under 6 years	ask a doctor

Other information Store at 2°-30° C (36°-86° F)
■ protect from excessive moisture

Inactive ingredients D&C yellow no. 10, lactose, magnesium stearate, microcrystalline cellulose, pregelatinized starch

Label not to scale

© 2002 KRT
Source: U.S. Food and Drug Administration
Graphic: Pai

In 2002, pharmaceutical companies revised the labels on all over-the-counter medications to follow FDA guidelines. The ingredients, side effects, and directions must be clearly listed on medicine bottles, and technical words such as "contraindications" can no longer be used to explain simple warnings. This label change affected more than 100,000 products in the United States.

will also have a warning if the drug can be dangerous for women who are pregnant or breastfeeding. There may also be a warning to keep the drug out of the reach of children.

DIRECTIONS
The label must give instructions for how to take the medication. Directions are usually based on a person's age. For example, a child will take less of the medicine than an adult. The directions will say how much of the medication to take, and how often.

(continues on page 30)

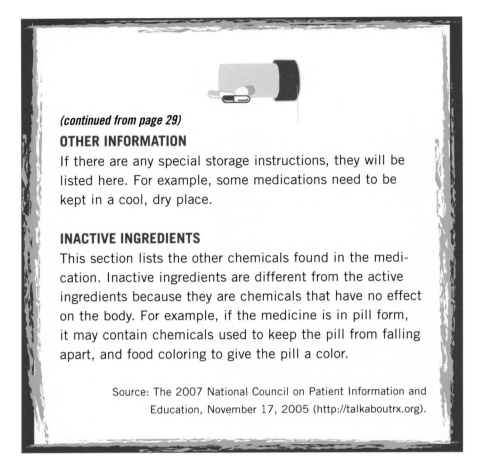

(continued from page 29)

OTHER INFORMATION

If there are any special storage instructions, they will be listed here. For example, some medications need to be kept in a cool, dry place.

INACTIVE INGREDIENTS

This section lists the other chemicals found in the medication. Inactive ingredients are different from the active ingredients because they are chemicals that have no effect on the body. For example, if the medicine is in pill form, it may contain chemicals used to keep the pill from falling apart, and food coloring to give the pill a color.

Source: The 2007 National Council on Patient Information and Education, November 17, 2005 (http://talkaboutrx.org).

(continued from page 27)
trend of OTC drug abuse among young people and the serious dangers of this abuse.

Today, nearly half of all OTC drugs have some amount of DXM in them. Not only are these drugs sold in stores, but they are also available on the Internet. Although many people are working to restrict the sale of drugs containing DXM, the level of abuse continues.

DXM: A DISSOCIATIVE DRUG

A **dissociative drug** is a drug that causes what are commonly referred to as out-of-body experiences, or hallucinations. When people use dissociative drugs, the chemicals in the drug block signals in the brain. These signals affect the conscious mind, or the part of the brain that tells the person what he or she is feeling. When the brain is deprived of these signals, the person can have hallucinations.

The most common dissociative drugs are phencyclidine (PCP), ketamine, DXM, and nitrous oxide (laughing gas). These drugs can also affect the **central nervous system**. The central nervous system controls the body's behavior. It is divided into two parts: the brain and the spinal cord. Dissociative drugs slow down the nervous system, which can cause it to not work properly. For example, these drugs can slow breathing and lower the heart rate. The effects are often described as intense feelings of being detached from yourself, feeling like your surroundings are strange or unreal, a foggy feeling, or a feeling of painlessness.

Using DXM to experience these dissociative effects is often called *robo tripping*, a reference to the cough medicine Robitussin. Some people compare robo tripping to the types of hallucinations people describe when they take the illegal drugs PCP or ketamine. Part of the draw to DXM is that, unlike PCP and ketamine, there is no law against purchasing or abusing the drug. However, although using DXM is legal, there are still laws against adults providing intoxicating doses to minors (people under age 18).

THE DANGERS OF ROBO TRIPPING

There are different stages, or "plateaus," a person reaches when robo tripping. These plateaus describe how high a person gets from using DXM. Plateaus can range from feeling mildly confused to having visual hallucinations and out-of-body experiences. How quickly a person reaches

DXM'S STREET NAMES

People often make up names for the drugs they abuse. These are commonly referred to as street names.

People use street names for drugs for different reasons. For example, using the street name makes it clear that a person is using the drug to get high, and not to treat a specific illness or symptom. Some people think it's cool to use street names to show their knowledge of the drug. They think using street names lets other people know that they are aware of the current slang. Sometimes people use street names so that other people who are not familiar with the slang won't know what they are talking about. For example, they may refer to DXM as "candy." New names for the same drug are often created as people catch on to a familiar term. Here are some of the most common street names for DXM:

- Candy
- CCC
- Dex
- Drex
- DM
- Red Devils
- Robo
- Rojo
- Skittles
- Syrup
- Triple C
- Tussin
- Velvet
- Vitamin D

different plateaus depends on how much DXM the person takes, how much the person weighs, and other factors.

The first plateau makes the person feel slightly **intoxicated**. For example, the person may feel slightly dizzy or lightheaded. The second plateau causes behaviors similar to being drunk: People may slur their words and have trouble walking normally or controlling their movements. Some people may have trouble remembering things and carrying on a conversation.

The third plateau is what DXM abusers often aim to reach. At this level, users have an out-of-body experience, or hallucinations. They lose control of their motor skills, which means they can't make their arms and legs move the way that they want. People often say they can't think straight, and lose track of where they are, or even *who* they are. The most dangerous plateau is the fourth plateau. At this point the person loses total control of his or her body and mind.

Each of these plateaus comes with serious risks, and the higher the plateau, the more dangerous. Some of the life-threatening risks include seizures and extremely high body temperatures, which can cause death. Another risk of using medicines to get high is that other ingredients in the medicine besides DXM can also have side effects. For example, antihistamines (allergy medicines) are also found in many of the medicines that have DXM. In high doses, these drugs can cause people to have irregular heartbeats, high blood pressure, and seizures. Taken over a long period of time, acetaminophen, found in Tylenol, can cause liver failure.

INCREASING THE RISK: TURNING LIQUID TO POWDER

Most people who abuse DXM take large doses of medications that have DXM in them. For example, they may take high doses of cough syrup or several pills at a time. Others have found a way to increase the effects of DXM by extracting (taking out) the ingredient from the medicines. By creating a powder form of DXM, users produce a much more potent level of the drug. Once they have the powder, they snort it or inhale it. Users get high more quickly, and reach higher plateaus. They often

"ROBO TRIPPING" AND OTHER STREET NAMES

Just as there are street names for DXM, there are also street names for *using* DXM. People make up these names for reasons similar to why they come up with names for the drug itself. They may want to give the impression that they are regular users, or they think they'll impress others if they know the slang to describe abusing drugs. Or they may not want parents or other adults to know what they're talking about. Some common street names for abusing OTC drugs include:

- Dexing
- Robo tripping
- Robo dosing
- Robo fizzing
- Robo-ing
- Skittling

Finally, "smurfing" is a term used to describe buying cough medicine from several different stores. Even people who abuse the drugs have a nickname: "syrup heads."

reach dangerous plateau levels by mistake, not realizing how powerful the drug is.

For these reasons, the powder form of DXM is highly dangerous. Since people began abusing DXM in pure powder form, availability of the drug has increased. Most users prefer the powder form because it's easier and faster to take than it is to swallow large doses of liquid medicine, which commonly causes vomiting. Another way people abuse DXM is by taking the powder form and mixing it with alcohol, marijuana, or **Ecstasy**. These drugs increase the effects to even more dangerous levels.

Although there are many Internet sites and online groups that share information on abusing DXM, there are also many sites devoted to sharing information about the real dangers. Because the Internet makes learning about abusing DXM so much easier for people of all ages, many believe the Food and Drug Administration should further restrict the online sale of the drug.

3

The Real Costs of OTC Abuse

Seven high school students in El Dorado, California, were rushed to the hospital in October 2006. Two of the students had complained that they were feeling sick to their stomachs late in the morning. Then five more students began to have similar symptoms: They had upset stomachs and were vomiting. All seven had overdosed on the nonprescription cough medicine Coricidin. The pills had been bought at a discount store.

An investigation uncovered the story. One girl had brought three boxes of the medication to school. Between morning classes, she shared the medicine in a school restroom with several other students. Each student swallowed five to eight tablets.

The students ended up being okay physically, but they paid a price for their actions. A sheriff involved in

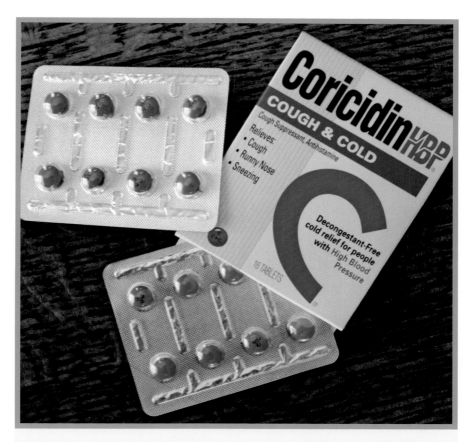

Manufactured as a cold medicine for people with high blood pressure, Coricidin is a widely abused over-the-counter drug. Also known as "Triple C's," this medication is easily attainable and contains DXM. Authorities have noticed Coricidin overdose incidents tend to occur in clusters, usually due to one person sharing several boxes of the drug with a group of friends.

the investigation told reporters that the student responsible for bringing the medication to school would face criminal charges. The school principal also said that the students who took the medication would be treated in the same way as students are treated for drinking alcohol or taking illegal drugs.

A QUICK HIGH

People who abuse drugs are often looking for a quick high. They look for drugs that are the easiest to get their hands on and that will take effect quickly when used. For young people who abuse drugs, this makes OTC drugs the most desirable. They are legal, fairly inexpensive, and often easy to get. But people who abuse drugs often don't think beyond the high they crave. They don't think about the possible short- or even long-term consequences of abusing drugs. Sometimes they may have been aware of the risks, but at some point they stopped caring. They crave the feeling of getting high so badly that they are willing to take the risks.

Side effects are the possible risks associated with taking a certain medication. A list of the known side effects for a medication is included on its label. Examples might include stomach pain, dizziness, drowsiness, trouble sleeping, or other uncomfortable results. Companies that distribute medications are required by law to list all of the known, possible side effects reported or revealed when the drug was tested.

There are different types of side effects. Some can be short-term effects, which means they are side effects the person might experience shortly after taking the medication. These last only for a short period of time—from several minutes or hours to a day or two. Long-term side effects are those that last long after the high is gone. These may be risks associated with the drug when the drug is taken over a long period of time, but that is not always the case. Sometimes people can suffer long-term side effects after abusing an OTC drug only one time. Both long- and short-term side effects can be serious and life threatening.

What many young people don't realize is that the side effects listed on OTC drug labels are possible side effects based on tests done when the recommended doses were taken. They are *not* the side effects that can occur when a drug is abused and higher amounts are taken. Users may read the label and think the drug sounds fairly harmless. But when someone doubles, triples, or takes even more of the recommended dosage of a drug, it is far more difficult to predict the short- and

A TRUE STORY OF LIVER FAILURE

On September 17, 2006, a 16-year-old girl died after swallowing 20 Coricidin pills. Lucia Martino lived in Anaheim, California. She was a soccer player and a junior in high school. One morning her mother woke up to find Lucia vomiting. Lucia was rushed to the emergency room. She went into a coma, and four days later she died of liver failure. At first, the doctors who were dealing with Lucia's death were confused about what could cause liver failure in such a young person. Finally, her friends came forward and told Lucia's nurse about the pills.

Lucia's death stunned the community and was considered a wake-up call about the real risks of OTC drug abuse. Soon after her death, the *Los Angeles Times* ran a story about the dangers of teens abusing cough medicine. The Parent Teacher Association from the Anaheim area schools formed a committee to help teach parents about teen OTC drug abuse, as well as other drug abuse. It's a small effort against a large problem, but many times, important movements start with a small group of people determined to make a change.

long-term side effects because these have not been tested as thoroughly.

THE PRICE OF CONTINUED USE

For people who abuse DXM over a long period of time, the effects can be significantly more damaging. One of the most serious is brain damage. This can happen after one use, or over a period of continued use.

COMMON SHORT-TERM SIDE EFFECTS OF DXM

Abusing drugs that contain DXM can cause death. Even if the result is not fatal, the following side effects may occur:

- Brain damage: This can occur due to a long period of use, as well as short-term use.
- Confusion or disorientation: The person may forget where he or she is or what time it is, for example.
- Dizziness: The person may also have blurred or double vision.
- Feeling very sleepy: The person may fall asleep or pass out.
- Hallucinations: The person may start to see things that aren't there, or feel like he or she is in a strange, unfamiliar place.
- Rapid heartbeat: This can be very dangerous, and even fatal.
- Heatstroke: The person may stop sweating, his or her body temperature may rise, and he or she

One common result of continued abuse of OTC drugs over a long period of time is liver damage. When the liver doesn't function properly, it can lead to all kinds of other serious health problems. The liver is the largest organ in the human body. It filters out toxic substances from the body, such as alcohol and medications. It also helps remove old or damaged red blood cells from the blood, and helps make it possible for blood to

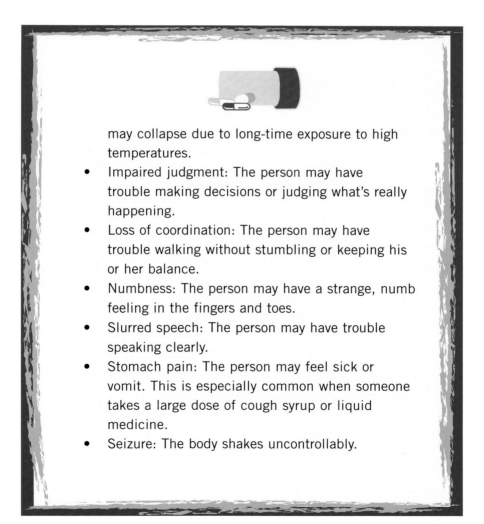

may collapse due to long-time exposure to high temperatures.

- Impaired judgment: The person may have trouble making decisions or judging what's really happening.
- Loss of coordination: The person may have trouble walking without stumbling or keeping his or her balance.
- Numbness: The person may have a strange, numb feeling in the fingers and toes.
- Slurred speech: The person may have trouble speaking clearly.
- Stomach pain: The person may feel sick or vomit. This is especially common when someone takes a large dose of cough syrup or liquid medicine.
- Seizure: The body shakes uncontrollably.

form clots to help the body stop bleeding. The liver also helps store vitamins, minerals, and proteins from your diet, and helps the intestines absorb and digest fats. When the liver becomes damaged, it has a harder time performing these functions the way it needs to in order to keep the body healthy. Acetaminophen, which is found in many OTC medications, is known to increase the risk of liver damage when taken over a period of time.

SOCIAL SIDE EFFECTS

Abusing OTC drugs also has many, often unforeseen, social side effects. Many people who abuse OTC drugs, like any other drug abusers, may start out using drugs with friends, or because their friends have pressured them to use. They may actually start abusing OTC drugs because they think it will improve their social status. Yet, as people continue to abuse drugs, they begin to put getting high above anything else, even friends. Often people start to withdraw from friends and family. They may also spend less and less time doing schoolwork, or doing their jobs well. Drug abuse can tear families apart.

TROUBLE WITH THE LAW

Another effect of continued drug abuse is trouble with the law. Even though OTC drugs tend to be much less expensive than illegal drugs, continued use adds up. People often turn to theft in order to get the drugs. They may attempt to steal the drugs from a store or from someone's home. They may also try to steal money in order to pay for the drugs. In addition, abusing any kind of drug often leads people to behave in ways they wouldn't if they were sober. They often take risks they normally wouldn't take or make choices that put them in danger. For example, people have been known to try reckless stunts while under the influence of drugs, or make dangerous choices about sex, or get in a car with someone they don't know. This happens because when people are under the influence, their judgment becomes impaired, or cloudy. They have trouble concentrating or thinking about the consequences of their decisions. Or they may feel so "good," they don't care what happens.

TRAPPED IN THE WEB

There are different theories about why OTC drug abuse is on the rise. Many people believe that the main reason is because these drugs are easier to get than illegal drugs. Also, since the drugs are legal, there isn't a risk of jail time for using them.

Another large contributor to OTC abuse is the Internet. There are many Web sites that seem to be run by knowledgeable experts giving out information on drug use. These people are not experts—they are simply drug abusers themselves. In addition, message forums allow abusers to share their experiences, which can make abusing OTC drugs seem like the thing "everyone" is doing. Popular sites such as MySpace and Facebook are other places people readily post their experiences about abusing OTC drugs.

There are also sites that post articles about OTC drugs and the dangers of abuse, and then make arguments about how these articles aren't accurate. The people who run these sites are not doctors and therefore don't have the knowledge needed to make informed decisions about OTC drug abuse. They are OTC abusers who put themselves and others in danger.

These sites are easily accessible to anyone with a computer and Internet access. Often, when one person hears about how someone got high using something they found right in their parents' medicine cabinet, the news travels quickly among friends and online

A CAUSE WORTH FIGHTING FOR

In addition to the law-making efforts described in the previous chapter, many parents and young people have begun to promote OTC drug awareness. There are many Web sites now devoted to educating people of all ages about the facts of OTC abuse, with particular attention paid to the health risks of DXM. These sites often have different sections for young people, parents, educators, and those who work in law enforcement.

Education is often considered the most effective tool to help prevent drug abuse. As more people become aware of the current trend and the dangers associated with OTC drug abuse, many believe the number of people abusing the drug will go down. Some people believe that drug users will always find ways to abuse drugs, whether the drugs are legal or not. Yet, others don't agree. They think that education and stricter access to the drugs will help prevent people from abusing them. Many also believe that less access to drugs will help prevent future overdoses.

Some drugstore owners have restricted certain areas in their stores, making medicines unavailable to people younger than 18. In addition, the Consumer Healthcare Products Association is pushing for laws to ban online sales of pure powdered DXM. The association also wants to try to shut down Web sites that promote DXM abuse.

communities. Soon, large groups of people are trying these drugs. What these sites don't often report are all the negative effects these drugs have. In fact, some

Here are some ways that other people can make a difference:

- Students can learn about the dangers of OTC drug abuse and communicate these dangers to others.
- Recovering abusers can give their own accounts about how abusing OTC drugs affected them, and they can post their stories on the Internet and in other public places.
- Teachers can educate themselves about the dangers of OTC drug abuse and learn what signs to look for to help any students who may be in trouble.
- Parents, like teachers, should learn how to prevent their children from abusing OTC drugs by learning the signs to watch for, as well as keeping track of the medicines they have available at home. Parents should also talk to their kids about illegal and OTC drug abuse.
- Anti-drug campaigns can also help. For example, The Partnership for a Drug-Free America now has specific information about OTC drug abuse on its Web site.

poison control centers say they notice groups of emergency calls happening in "pockets" or regions. They believe this happens because, as word spreads about the drugs in different communities, groups of people are trying the drugs at about the same time—and overdosing.

The Internet can be a wonderful tool to gain information, but not all information is accurate or reliable. Web sites can be designed to look very official and authoritative, when in reality, anyone can design a Web site and post whatever information—true or not—on that site. There are no authorities to stop a person from sharing incorrect and dangerous information.

4

Cough Medicine: The Most Commonly Abused OTC Drug

Carl Hennos seemed to be a typical teenager. He loved to play the guitar and was considered a gifted player. He applied and was accepted to the Memphis College of Art and planned to attend in the fall of 2003. One morning, the summer before Carl was to start college, his mom woke up early to walk their dog. She decided to let Carl and his brother sleep rather than wake them before she left. But when she returned, Carl still wasn't awake. When she tried to wake him, she knew something wasn't right. He wasn't moving. Carl's mother was a trained nurse and tried to give him CPR, but he was already dead.

How could a healthy young man suddenly die in his sleep? What his mom didn't know at that moment was that Carl wasn't as healthy as she thought. He was a regular cough medicine abuser. He died in his sleep from an overdose of the cough syrup Robitussin. Carl was only 18 years old and had been abusing the cough syrup for two and a half years, but his mom had no idea.

HOW COUGH MEDICINE WORKS

There are two different types of cough medicines. One type is called an **expectorant**. The other is called an **antitussive**. Each one has a distinct way to treat a cough.

When someone has a cold with a cough, mucus and other substances block the air tubes that go to the lungs. Expectorants work by thinning the mucus that's blocking the lungs, making it easier to cough up. This makes coughing more "productive," because when the mucus is thinner, it's easier to cough up. An active ingredient in OTC expectorants is **guaifenesin**. Expectorant medications that have guaifenesin in them have very few side effects when taken as directed (meaning when one follows the directions on the label). Possible side effects include trouble sleeping, upset stomach, and rash.

ABUSE IS SPREADING

According to The Partnership for a Drug-Free America, 1 out of 10 teens in the United States abused cough medicine in 2005. That's more than 2 million teens across the country. Of all the OTC drugs on the market, cough medicine is one of the most heavily abused.

Antitussive cough medicines are cough suppressants. A suppressant is something that causes an action to stop. Cough suppressants send signals to the area in the brain that controls the cough reflex. In other words, an antitussive tricks a person's brain into thinking that he or she doesn't need to cough. Cough suppressants are for relieving dry, hacking, irritating coughs. They aren't meant to stop the productive type of coughing needed to help clear mucus and phlegm from the lungs. People can also use cough suppressants to treat chronic coughs caused by other lung problems, such as those caused by smoking, asthma, or the lung disease emphysema. DXM is a common ingredient in antitussive medications.

MILLIONS HAVE TRIED IT

In December 2006, the *Los Angeles Times* reported that the practice of "robo tripping" on cough medicine was rising by 50% each year. According to the article, recent studies have shown that the abuse of illegal drugs such as LSD, GHB, and Ecstasy is going down, while the abuse of OTC medicines is on the rise. The report showed that two-thirds of the people who abuse OTC drugs abuse Coricidin HBP Cough & Cold. The medicine comes in small red tablets that look like candy. Some common street names for the medicine are "triple C," "CCC," and "skittles."

Coricidin isn't the only drug being abused. With more than a hundred OTC cough medicines containing DXM, people have easy access to the drug in many forms. Some of these medicines have DXM as the only active ingredient, while others combine DXM with other chemicals. Many cough medicines are combined with other medicines in this way to treat more than one symptom. For example, a medicine might have an ingredient to suppress coughs, as well as other ingredients to treat a fever, headache, or runny nose.

Abusing cough medicine means a person takes more than the recommended dose to get high or to experience other effects from taking too much medicine. Some abusers take 25 to 50 times the recommended dose—as many as 80 cough medicine pills a day. For those who

COUGH MEDICINES THAT CONTAIN DXM

There are more than 100 different OTC drugs that contain DXM as the only active ingredient, or combine DXM with other active ingredients. Some common name brands include:

- Alka-Seltzer Plus Cold & Cough Medicine
- Contac
- Coricidin HBP Cough and Cold
- Dayquil LiquiCaps
- Dimetapp DM
- Musinex DM
- PediaCare cough medicines
- Robitussin cough products
- Sudafed cough products
- Theraflu cold and flu products
- Triaminic cough syrups
- Tylenol Cold products
- Vicks 44 Cough Relief products
- Vicks NyQuil LiquiCaps
- Zicam

abuse cough syrup rather than pills, this means drinking one or more entire bottles of cough medicine. People often mix the syrup with alcohol, which increases the dangers significantly since many cough and cold medicines have warnings *not* to mix them with alcohol or certain drugs.

Another dangerous trend is called "pharming." This is the name used for bringing lots of pills to a party and sharing them with friends. Here's how it works: Someone has a party at his or her house. As each person arrives, they put whatever pills they brought into a bowl. When it's time to start, all the pills in the bowl are mixed together. Then the bowl gets passed around and each person takes a handful of the pills. The pills are usually swallowed down with soda or alcohol. Then everyone waits for the results to take effect.

Robo pharming is extremely dangerous. People who do this have no idea what pills they are taking, or where the pills came from. Anyone could slip any sort of pill they wanted into the bowl and no one would know what it was. In addition, taking a mixture of pills that are not supposed to be combined could have serious and deadly side effects.

THE LURE OF COUGH MEDICINE

The reason cough medicine is the most abused of all the over-the-counter drugs available is probably because DXM is the main ingredient in most OTC cough medicines. Another reason is that people have a choice in how to take it: Since cough medicine comes in many different forms, someone who doesn't like taking cough syrup can take the pills instead, and vice versa.

As with any drug, there are a number of reasons why people abuse cough medicine. On the Web site "Make Up Your Own Mind About Cough Medicine" (www.

dxmstories.com), which is part of The Partnership for a Drug-Free America, there are several testimonials by young people who have abused cough medicine and other OTC drugs. Many of them say that they first tried getting high with cough medicine just for fun. They describe the strange hallucinations they had and their

DRUG USE IN MIDDLE SCHOOL AND HIGH SCHOOL

The Partnership for a Drug-Free America surveyed middle school and high school students about their drug use. The organization then published the results showing what percentage of students had tried which drugs. Here are the results:

Marijuana: 37%
Inhalants (products people sniff the fumes of to get high): 20%
Prescription medicine (that had not been prescribed to them): 19%
Cough medicine: 10%
Cocaine/crack: 10%
Methamphetamine: 8%
Ecstasy: 8%
LSD: 6%
Heroin: 5%
Ketamine: 4%
GHB: 4%

Source: The Partnership for a Drug-Free America

inability to control their bodies. Although OTC cough medicine is not considered addictive, many people come to rely on the drug's effects. These people often say they just wanted to "feel numb."

THE HIDDEN DANGERS

Like all legal OTC medicine, cough medicine is carefully tested and labeled with instructions on how much medicine to take and how often to take it. These strict labeling guidelines were developed for a reason: to keep people safe.

Yet, the risks of cough medicine abuse aren't just related to taking too much of the drug. How often a person takes it can cause problems, too. Like most medicines, cough medicines aren't meant to be taken daily over a long period of time. Most medicine labels say not to take the drug for more than 48 hours, or some other limited amount of time. This is because the chemical ingredients are strong and can have negative effects on the body and its organs if taken too long.

A person is also taking severe risks when swallowing large doses of these drugs with other medicines or with alcohol. For example, when DXM is combined with medicines containing acetaminophen, there is an increased risk of liver damage, heart attack, stroke, and death. Acetaminophen is found in many OTC medicines. When people take large amounts, it can cause major damage to the liver. Although the liver can slowly heal over time, it is still a very serious health risk to damage it.

In 2006, the University of North Carolina at Chapel Hill studied the pain reliever Tylenol (which contains acetaminophen) and its effect on the liver. The study found that 31% to 44% of the people who took Tylenol for 14 days in a row showed signs of possible liver

The liver is a vital organ, and people who abuse drugs and alcohol can suffer from liver scarring. A healthy liver *(left)* will produce enzymes to help the body digest and process food, while also filtering out the toxins in the bloodstream. Those with extensive liver scarring and tissue damage *(right)*—whether from drinking, drug abuse, or liver disease—tend to suffer from nosebleeds, jaundice, and severe pains. (The middle image shows a fatty liver.)

damage. Based on their study, researchers warned the public that acetaminophen could cause liver damage, particularly scarring, in as little as four days.

Liver damage is serious because this organ is essential in fighting infection and diseases. When people have damaged livers, they are at a higher risk of getting sick. The more damaged the liver becomes, the greater the risk. When the liver is damaged over and over, it starts to scar. The scar tissue replaces healthy liver tissue, and over time the scar tissue keeps the liver from doing its job.

SIDE EFFECTS OF COUGH MEDICINE ABUSE

The side effects of cough medicine abuse are similar to those of other products that contain DXM. They include:

- Blurred vision
- Confusion
- Drowsiness
- Itchy skin caused by rashes
- Memory problems
- Nausea and vomiting
- Numbness in the toes and fingers
- Panic attacks
- Rapid heartbeat
- Slurred speech
- Unconsciousness

Whether it's cough medicine or any other OTC drug, abuse of over-the-counter medicine is considered a quickly growing problem in the United States. However, many believe that more efforts will be made to help prevent OTC drug abuse once more people become aware of the dangers.

5

Other Commonly Abused OTC Drugs

Cough medicine may be one of the most commonly abused OTC drugs, but it certainly isn't the only one. People abuse all kinds of OTC drugs, including pain relievers, cold and allergy medicines, diet pills, sleep aids, motion sickness medications, bodybuilding drugs, herbal medications, caffeine pills and drinks, and others. A lot of people may not even consider the drugs they are taking to be "drugs." For example, some people may not think caffeine is really an over-the-counter drug. But it is. Energy drinks loaded with caffeine have become an increasing concern as more and more young people become addicted to them. Some schools have made rules for what types of beverages can be sold in vending machines, in the hopes that this will prevent students from taking in too much caffeine. Many schools also have rules that prevent students from bringing any medications to school without special permission.

PAIN RELIEVERS

Pain relievers help treat symptoms such as headaches, sore throat, injuries, and other aches and pains. People may also be given OTC pain relievers after surgery, instead of prescription medications, which can be much stronger. Most pain relievers are known as nonsteroidal anti-inflammatory drugs, or NSAIDS. Common NSAIDS include aspirin, acetaminophen, and ibuprofen.

Some drugs come from plants. For example, aspirin originally came from willow plants. There are also newer, synthetic pain relievers. The word *synthetic* describes a substance that was made by people, often in a laboratory. Some examples of synthetic medicines are ibuprofen, acetaminophen, and naproxen. In addition to treating pain, these synthetic NSAIDS also help reduce swelling (called inflammation) and fever. Some pain relievers are combined with another drug to treat multiple symptoms. For example, some medications treat pain and fever as well as other cold symptoms.

OTC pain relievers are not meant to be taken on an ongoing basis. Often the warning label will tell people not to take them for more than a specific number of days. One of the dangers of taking NSAIDs for too long is that they can damage a person's stomach. They can cause ulcers in the stomach or intestinal lining. Sometimes these ulcers bleed, or create a hole that can break through the stomach or intestinal wall. This can lead to heavy blood loss, which may require an emergency blood transfusion. In some cases, it can even cause death.

As has been discussed, certain NSAIDs can also cause liver damage. Studies have shown that people who take acetaminophen for more than four days in a row are at an increased risk. Continued use or abuse of NSAIDS can also cause kidney damage.

ASPIRIN ABUSE

Aspirin is used to treat aches and pains and to reduce fever. But aspirin can be very dangerous to children and teens. This is because aspirin has been known to cause Reye's syndrome, a condition that affects the brain, liver, and other organs. Reye's syndrome can cause severe vomiting and swelling of the brain and liver. It can also cause mental problems, and even death. Children and teens at risk are those who may have the flu or chicken pox when they take aspirin.

Some signs of an overdose of aspirin include:

- Burning in the throat or stomach
- Fever
- Confusion
- Decrease in urination
- Dizziness
- Hallucination
- Loss of consciousness
- Seizures
- Shaking
- Sleepiness
- Vomiting

COLD, FLU, AND ALLERGY MEDICINES

People abuse OTC cold and flu remedies often because they contain DXM to control coughing. They may also abuse them for other ingredients, such as pain relievers, which can produce similar highs.

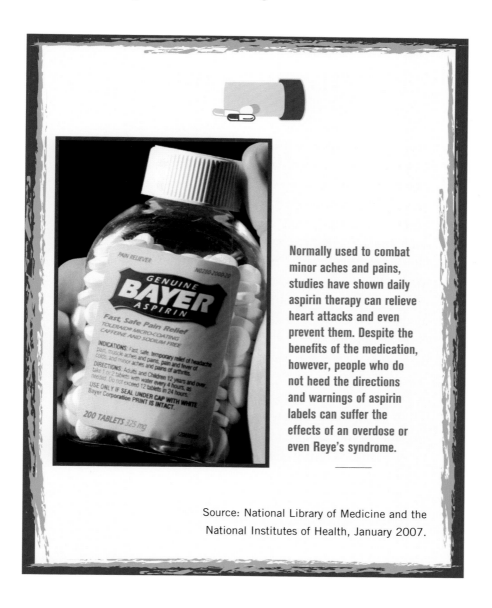

Normally used to combat minor aches and pains, studies have shown daily aspirin therapy can relieve heart attacks and even prevent them. Despite the benefits of the medication, however, people who do not heed the directions and warnings of aspirin labels can suffer the effects of an overdose or even Reye's syndrome.

Source: National Library of Medicine and the National Institutes of Health, January 2007.

There are more than a hundred OTC drugs for helping to relieve the symptoms of colds and allergies. But these drugs treat only the symptoms, not the illness itself. Viruses are what cause colds and the flu, and OTC

ACETAMINOPHEN ABUSE

Acetaminophen is a pain reliever that usually does not have any side effects. It is usually used to treat headaches or muscle pain, such as a backache. Acetaminophen can also be taken to help lower a fever. It is considered safe when taken as instructed on the label. But if a person takes acetaminophen in large doses, he or she may vomit, have unusual bleeding or bruising, have severe stomach pain, and other symptoms. If the person has a kidney or liver problem, it is dangerous to take acetaminophen without talking with a doctor first. Common brand names of medicines that have acetaminophen include Tylenol, Midol, and Excedrin.

Some signs of an overdose of acetaminophen include:

- Bleeding or bruising
- Extreme tiredness
- Flu-like symptoms
- Nausea or vomiting
- Sweating
- Yellowing of the skin or eyes

Source: National Library of Medicine and the National Institutes of Health, January 2007.

drugs do not fight viruses. They can help a person feel better while they have the illness, but they don't make the illness go away. Time and the body's natural disease-fighting system do that.

Often, OTC cold and flu "remedies" have a combination of chemicals to treat several symptoms, such as a headache, cough, and runny nose. A lot of times, people may take an OTC cold medicine that treats several cold symptoms, even if they only have one of these symptoms. For this reason, people often take more drugs than they really need. For example, if a person has a stuffy nose but not a cough, he or she shouldn't take a medicine labeled "cough and cold." In order to make

IBUPROFEN ABUSE

Ibuprofen is another pain reliever that may be abused. In addition to pain, ibuprofen can be used to help treat arthritis and lower a fever. Abusing ibuprofen can cause confusion, vomiting, and a tingling feeling in the hands and feet. Common brand names of medicines that have ibuprofen include Advil and Motrin.

Some signs of an overdose of ibuprofen include:

- Blue lips, mouth and nose
- Dizziness
- Rapid, uncontrollable eye movements

Source: National Library of Medicine and the National Institutes of Health, January 2007.

the safest choice, people should read the label on the medication and make sure they take a medication that only treats their particular symptoms.

Just as cold and flu medicines don't cure the illness, OTC allergy medicines do not destroy allergens, either. Allergens cause a release of **histamines**, a chemical that is produced naturally in the body. A histamine's job is to help heal the body from illness or injury. But in the case of allergies, the body produces too much histamine. This causes a stuffy or runny nose, sneezing, itchy throat, watery eyes, and coughing, among other problems. These are all common signs of allergies. OTC allergy medicines help tone down the body's reaction to the allergens in order to make daily life with them more comfortable. For example, OTC allergy medications may work to keep the nose from running or eyes from itching. The active ingredient in most OTC allergy medicines is an antihistamine. An antihistamine tells the body to produce less histamine, making the symptoms less severe.

DIET PILLS

People hoping to control or lose weight have used diet pills for many years. Appetite suppressants, or drugs that make you feel like you aren't hungry, are a common type of diet pill. But like other OTC drugs, some people abuse this type of drug. There are different reasons for diet pill abuse. Some young people take diet pills because they think they'll lose weight quickly, and they often don't heed warning labels. Taking diet pills to lose weight can be extremely dangerous. For example, people with eating disorders may take diet pills to try to lose weight when they are already severely underweight. This causes even more health problems.

Another reason people may take diet pills is for the high that the ingredients in some diet pills can produce.

Fen-phen, a prescription diet drug, was pulled from the market when doctors discovered a possible link between the medication and serious, sometimes fatal, conditions such as heart valve disease and pulmonary hypertension. About 18 million Americans had taken fen-phen before the FDA finally pulled it from the market in 1997. Patricia Buol *(shown with her husband, Jeff)* developed serious heart problems after taking fen-phen, and had to then live with a catheter (*shown on the table*) directly connected to her heart.

But again, often this means taking more than the recommended dose, which can be very dangerous, even deadly.

Until recently, many OTC appetite suppressants contained **phenylpropanolamine** (PPA) and caffeine. These are similar to amphetamines, a drug only available by prescription. PPA is a stimulant, meaning it speeds up the central nervous system. Some well-known diet pills that once contained PPA include Acutrim, Dexatrim,

Protrim, and Dietac. These drugs were especially unsafe for young people, and when taken in higher doses or for a longer time than recommended, they were not safe for anyone. In 2005, the FDA ordered that all OTC drugs containing phenylpropanolamine be taken out of stores.

The side effects of PPA included dizziness, sleepless-ness, and an irregular heartbeat. These side effects were possible even when taking the directed amount of the drug. If someone took more than the recommended dose, the results were even more serious. Risks of abus-ing diet pills with PPA include:

- Chest pain
- Violent and uncontrollable muscle spasms
- Diarrhea
- High blood pressure
- Irregular heartbeat
- Rash

Another dangerous ingredient that was once used in some OTC diet pills was **ephedrine.** It is now consid-ered an extremely dangerous diet pill ingredient. Risks of ephedrine include:

- Anxiety
- Chest pain
- Dizziness
- Headaches
- Heart attack
- Nausea
- Rapid heartbeat
- Trouble breathing
- Death

Like phenylpropanolamine, the FDA ordered that ephedrine be taken out of stores. However, many OTC diet pill companies still put similar chemicals (with many similar side effects) in their pills.

Laxatives are another type of OTC drug that are sometimes abused by people trying to lose weight. Laxatives are meant to treat a person who is constipated, meaning that he or she is not able to naturally have a bowel movement. People who think they need to lose weight may take laxatives because they believe it will help them lose weight quickly. But laxatives do not cause real weight loss. That's because by the time food reaches the intestinal area, all the calories from the food have been taken in by the body.

Abusing laxatives is very dangerous. Some risks include:

- Chronic constipation (always being constipated)
- Dehydration, which can be deadly
- Heart attack
- Loss of control of the rectum, which leads to chronic diarrhea
- Nausea and vomiting
- Permanent bowel damage
- Severe stomach pain
- Death

Diuretics are another kind of OTC drug abused by people trying to lose weight quickly. These drugs make a person urinate heavily. The person may feel like he or she is losing weight, but actually the body is simply losing vital fluids that it must get back in order to be healthy again. Risks of diuretics are similar to those of laxatives. They include:

- Dehydration
- Heart failure
- Kidney damage
- Liver damage
- Death

The best way to reach a healthy weight is to eat healthy foods and get regular exercise. Many diet pills and other diet "aides" do not actually do anything that causes weight loss. The ones that might provide some help are considered a temporary help only.

BODYBUILDING SUPPLEMENTS

If you visit a fitness store, you may see many types of protein drinks and other "bodybuilding" supplements that are available without a prescription. Some people purchase these vitamins and supplements because they think it will help them build muscle and strength. People might abuse these drugs in order to achieve a certain weight. But as is the case with diet pills, laxatives, and diuretics, these drugs are abused to achieve an imagined idea of a perfect body. The FDA does not usually control these types of supplements, and so the risks aren't always known. This is why they are dangerous when abused, and particularly dangerous for younger people who are usually smaller than the average adult.

SLEEP AIDS

Sleep aids are medicines used to help people get a good night's rest if they are having trouble sleeping. In some cases, sleep aids have also been used to treat anxiety. They are not meant to be taken over a long period of time, and they are meant to be taken exactly as directed.

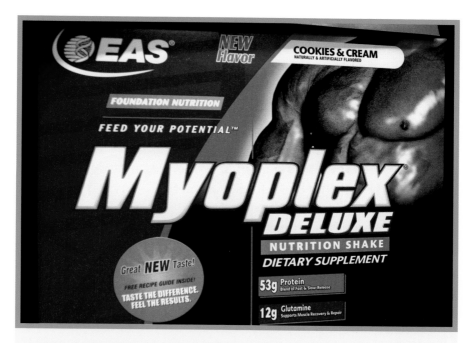

Dietary and exercise supplements are not held to the same standards as prescription or OTC medications. Used to enhance workouts or athletic performances, these supplements do not undergo medical testing before they are sold in stores. They are typically only removed from the market after serious health problems are reported to the FDA.

OTC sleep aids contain a kind of antihistamine that helps a person feel drowsy. Common OTC sleep aids include Sominex, Unisom, and Tylenol PM. Sleep aids can cause extreme dizziness and sleepiness. Abusing them can also lead to a condition called **narcolepsy**, which is a sleep disorder in which people have trouble with their sleep patterns or sometimes suddenly fall into periods of deep sleep.

Sleep aids are another OTC drug that is dangerous when abused. Some people abuse sleep medicine because it can make them delirious. People describe the feeling as being awake but in a dream-like state. But like all medicines, when someone takes too much, it can have serious side effects. These include:

- Blurred vision
- Confusion
- Constipation
- Extreme drowsiness
- Hallucinations
- Heart attack
- Irregular heart beat
- Rapid heart beat
- Sensitivity to bright light
- Twitching
- Death

MOTION SICKNESS MEDICATIONS

OTC motion sickness medicines are used to help prevent nausea and dizziness. People may take them before going on a long plane, train, car, or boat ride. Some people also take them before going on amusement park rides.

Some people also abuse OTC motion sickness pills. When taken in large amounts, the pills can cause hallucinations. But taking the amount of pills needed to reach that stage has serious side effects.

The chemical diphenhydramine is found in some OTC motion sickness medications. It is an antihistamine used to treat hay fever and allergies, and in some cases it may also be used to help with sleep. Diphenhydramine comes in different forms. It can be a tablet, capsule, or liquid. The chemical can be dangerous and is not recommended for children under the age of six. Side effects of diphenhydramine include:

- Headache
- Muscle weakness

- Nervousness
- Vision problems
- Trouble breathing
- Trouble urinating

Some common brand names of motion sickness medicines that contain diphenhydramine include Benadryl and Sominex.

HERBAL MEDICATIONS

Another type of medicine available over the counter is herbal medication. Some herbal medications treat the symptoms of colds and flu, headaches, and allergies. Some work as appetite suppressants, laxatives, or diuretics. Like other OTC drugs, people often think these drugs must be safe if they can be purchased without a prescription, and especially because these drugs are "natural." Still, many of these drugs can cause health risks if taken in large quantities. And, unlike other OTC drugs, the FDA does not regulate many herbal medicines. This means that a person can never be sure of an herbal medicine's safety.

CAFFEINE

Caffeine, a stimulant, is a natural drug found in plants. It can also be produced artificially. Caffeine is found in many OTC products, in addition to sports and energy drinks, and soft drinks. Caffeine is considered a drug because it affects the central nervous system by increasing heart rate and alertness.

A lot of people think that taking caffeine helps them feel more alert. But taking too much can have negative side effects, such as dizziness, headaches, and sleep problems. The other problem with caffeine is that it is addictive. When the body gets used to a regular dose of

Large amounts of caffeine and other energy-boosting chemicals are being added to drinks and even sunflower seeds *(above)*, but the FDA does not regulate these potentially harmful products. Marketed to young adults as a staple of a busy lifestyle, these new caffeine products may contain double the amount of caffeine in a cup of coffee and may be mixed with various stimulants that can produce negative side effects.

caffeine, a person goes through withdrawal when the intake stops. Caffeine withdrawal symptoms include headaches, muscle aches, depression, and moodiness. In addition, someone who takes caffeine on a regular basis gradually needs more caffeine to get the same effects.

Drinks that have caffeine can also cause dehydration, even though the body is taking in liquid. That's because caffeine increases the need to urinate, which empties the body of fluids.

OTC DRUGS: BIG BUSINESS

It seems to some that as long as there are OTC drugs available, someone will find a way to abuse them. Since the OTC drug industry is an extremely profitable business, it isn't likely that all OTC drugs that can be abused will be taken out of stores. Instead, people who want to protect others from being hurt by OTC drug abuse must continue to help educate the public about the dangers.

6

Why Do Young People Abuse Drugs?

The first time Shawn abused OTC drugs, he said he couldn't even walk. But he still liked the feeling. He liked the way the drugs relaxed him. Pretty soon, the drugs were all he cared about. He said he ended up breaking into cars and robbing people, just to get money to buy the drugs. People became afraid of him. Now that he's stopped, Shawn says it's hard to look back at his life and think about all the people he hurt and the things that he lost. He decided to tell the world his story so that people could hear firsthand what it was like to become an OTC drug addict. Shawn was videotaped giving his story, which was posted on The Partnership for a Drug-Free America Web site, www.dxmstories.com.

When the Food and Drug Administration finds that a prescription drug is safe, effective, and able to treat symptoms that can be self-diagnosed, the FDA changes the drug's status to make it available over the counter. Once a drug becomes available over the counter, more drug companies are allowed to produce the drug. This means that there will be more competition to sell the drug, and the price will go down. Even though they are less expensive than prescription drugs, OTC drugs are a billion-dollar industry in the United States. According to the National Center for Policy and Analysis, Americans spend about $20 billion on OTC drugs every year. Lower prices mean that more people can afford to buy OTC drugs, but that also means more people can afford to abuse them.

Young people give many reasons for abusing OTC drugs. Many say they do it for the thrill, or for laughs. Some do it because they are curious about what it will feel like. Others dare one another to get higher and higher. This chapter discusses some of the reasons that people—especially young people—choose to abuse over-the-counter drugs.

PEER PRESSURE

When you hear the term *peer pressure*, you probably already have a strong sense of what it means. You may think it refers to when people your age pressure you to use drugs or do something dangerous. You would be right. But peer pressure isn't always a bad thing.

Peer pressure is simply when people your age pressure you to do something. When peer pressure is used to encourage good behavior, people often refer to it as "positive peer pressure." Positive peer pressure can be many things. If you've ever encouraged a friend to join a sport with you, or to take up a new interest, that's positive peer pressure. And when a group of your friends all read the same book and tell you that you *have* to

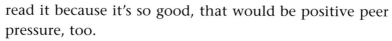

read it because it's so good, that would be positive peer pressure, too.

Peer pressure isn't something that only happens when you are young. Adults pressure one another, too. For example, coworkers may pressure one another to help work on a project, or to set new goals for the end of the year. Your parents' friends may have pressured them to join a book club, try a new restaurant, take up a new hobby, or go away on a combined family vacation.

On the other hand, pressuring friends to do something that isn't healthy, that is dangerous, or that could get them into trouble is negative peer pressure. Negative peer pressure happens to people of all ages. For young people, negative peer pressure usually means doing things that seem to be something that "everyone" is doing, or that seems cool. These can include trying alcohol or other drugs, cheating, skipping school, riding bikes or skateboarding without a helmet, and shoplifting. Adults may also experience negative peer pressure. For example, some adults may be pressured by their friends to go to a bar after work and drink before driving home. Or they may feel pressured by coworkers to put in extra hours in the office, even though they need a break.

For some people, it's hard to resist pressure from friends and other people their age. They may not have the courage they need to resist when friends ask them to do something they don't want to, or that they know is wrong. Resisting peer pressure can be especially hard for people who feel like they don't have many friends. They may think that doing what others are doing will help them be more popular. Or when a person has a low opinion of himself or herself (low **self-esteem**), he or she may not think taking risks matters. That's because people with very low self-esteem often don't care enough about themselves to make healthy and safe decisions.

Many young people who have abused OTC drugs say that the first time they tried them was with friends. But many people who then continued to abuse the drugs say they did so alone. As they began to feel their need for the drugs increase, they used the drugs more often—not just at parties, but also before and after school at their own homes.

TRYING TO ESCAPE

Anther common reason people turn to drug abuse is to escape problems. Although it doesn't make sense to think that using drugs will magically make problems go away, many people often say, "I just wanted to feel numb," or "I just wanted to forget about my problems for a little while" when they explain why they used drugs. Often when people are dealing with tough issues at home or at school, they feel hopeless and/or helpless. They think getting high is like taking a vacation from their problems. Unfortunately, not only do their problems not go away, but using drugs usually makes those problems even worse.

There are many things that people count as worries they need to "escape" from. One common school problem is bullying. Sometimes when people are being teased or hurt at school, they begin to feel bad about themselves. They may feel angry, too. They may then turn to drugs to make themselves feel like they have control over something—in this case, what they do to their body (even though the effect of the drug can make them lose control). School problems also include feeling like you don't fit in. People who have trouble making friends may feel alone and will turn to drugs because they think it will make them feel better.

Various problems at home are another common reason young people turn to drugs. There are many reasons someone might be having trouble at home. For example, a person may have parents who are always at work and never home. The person may feel bored or lonely and turn to drugs to get back at his or her parents, or to feel less lonely. Other people may have parents who constantly fight. In some cases, the fights might be physical. The person may start using drugs to "get away" from his or her surroundings. The person may think the drugs will help him or her feel numb to what's going on. Other people may be abused at home, either physically (being hit, for example) or verbally (being called names or being insulted). They may turn to drugs to try to numb their physical and emotional pain.

EMOTIONAL AND PSYCHOLOGICAL PROBLEMS

Another common reason people turn to drugs is because of emotional problems. People with emotional problems may think that getting high will make them feel better, or make it easier to deal with their feelings and problems. Some people have a mental illness, such as depression. They may not realize they have a real health problem. Instead, they turn to drugs to help them with their pain. Unfortunately, this only leads to more problems, both physical and emotional.

BODY IMAGE

Other people may abuse OTC drugs to try to alter their bodies in some way. For example, some people abuse diet pills, laxatives, and diuretics in order to lose weight quickly. People with an eating disorder may take

Girls are usually associated with eating disorders, but a growing number of boys are trying to attain the "perfect body" through unhealthy diet and exercise regimes. Males currently make up 10% of eating disorder cases in the United States and are more driven to control their weight for competitive sports. Laxatives and dietary supplements are often incorrectly used to maintain weight and muscle in sports, such as wrestling and bodybuilding.

these drugs in an attempt to "get rid" of any food they may have eaten. These are serious and deadly eating disorders.

People also abuse some OTC bodybuilding drugs to help them build muscle. They may think they will be more popular and make certain sports teams if they are a certain weight. Some sports, such as wrestling, require athletes to be a certain weight, because that determines the weight category in which they compete. Some athletes may try to lose or gain weight quickly so that they can be in the division they want. This can be extremely dangerous, since gaining or losing weight too quickly can make a person very sick.

SCHOOL AND SPORTS PERFORMANCE

People may also abuse OTC drugs that have high levels of caffeine and can cause a person to feel awake or have energy. Some people who are worried about their grades take drugs that keep them awake so they can stay up and study all night. Others may take the drugs to help them stay awake during school. Eventually, lack of sleep does catch up to people. They may have headaches, feel sick to their stomachs, get dizzy, and even end up falling asleep in class.

Some people take caffeinated energy drinks to help them have more energy while playing sports. But taking in too much of these drinks can be dangerous because they can also cause the body to become dehydrated. When people play sports and don't drink enough water, they are already becoming dehydrated through sweat, so energy drinks can make the problem even worse.

Taking too much caffeine can have other health effects as well. For example, it can cause anxiety, dizziness, and headaches. If you take caffeine for a long period of time and then stop, you can go through withdrawal symptoms, such as muscle aches, headaches, and even temporary depression.

TAKING RISKS

Another reason people abuse drugs is because they like to take risks. People have lots of reasons for taking risks. They may want to try to prove something to themselves—for example, that they aren't afraid of something. Destructive risk-taking is often connected to emotional problems. When it comes to abusing OTC drugs, people will commonly challenge each other to try to reach higher plateaus. For example, they may urge someone to take more pills than he or she ever has. This also ties in with peer pressure.

There are plenty of other examples of negative risks. Anything that is illegal is a negative risk. Putting yourself in danger or doing something unhealthy is also a negative risk. Some people may try unsafe stunts on their skateboard or bike, for example. Some may take risks by not following other safety rules, such as rules for driving. There are many stories of tragic accidents and deaths that have resulted from people taking dangerous risks.

Just like with peer pressure, not all risk-taking is negative. For example, a person may consider asking someone out on a date or trying out for a sports team as a risk. Other risks can include performing in front of an audience, or showing a friend a story that you've written. When people prepare themselves for a risk's outcome and are looking forward to a positive reward, risks like these can be considered positive risks.

JUST FOR FUN?

It's hard to imagine how someone can think it's fun to lose total control of his body, throw up, pass out, and forget where he or she is. But many people say one reason they try abusing OTC drugs is for the fun of it, or to relieve boredom. Many people confuse doing dangerous and unhealthy things with things that are actually fun. They forget that there are better ways to spend time and avoid boredom, ways that don't carry such dangerous risks.

Often, people don't think of the consequences of trying drugs, especially if they think the drug isn't dangerous or addictive. But many people who thought they would try "just once" have become regular abusers. Some have even died from abusing OTC drugs.

7

When and How to Get Help

Hannah was once considered the best player on her soccer team. She had the middle school record for number of goals scored in one season. One weekend, her friends invited her to a sleepover. One of the girls brought a new bottle of cold medicine pills. Another three brought full bottles of cough syrup. That night, the girls made up games for drinking the cough syrup and taking the pills. They mixed the pills with chocolate milk. Hannah liked the strange feeling the pills gave her. She felt like nothing mattered. She forgot about soccer and the pressure she often felt to be the best. A few days later after a soccer game, Hannah was in the bathroom at home. She opened the medicine cabinet and saw a new box of cold medicine. She took several pills and then went to her room. Once again, she felt the numbness.

She decided to take some more pills to school with her the next day. It wasn't long before Hannah was hooked.

Does the above story seem easy to believe? Even though it's fictional, this is based on several stories reported in the news—stories about how one night of OTC drug abuse led to a daily habit.

DOES YOUR FRIEND HAVE A PROBLEM?

Some people are very good at hiding the fact that they abuse drugs. Often someone goes from occasionally trying OTC drugs with friends to abusing the drugs on a regular basis, to abusing them frequently and often alone and in secret. They may have had fun experimenting with the drugs at first, but once they realize they are dependent on the drug, they may become ashamed and try to hide how often they abuse it.

If you think you know someone who might be abusing drugs, but you aren't sure, there are some signs that could give you a better idea. The following problems are common signs of drug abuse and addiction, but they could also be signs of other problems, such as depression.

Withdrawal from family and friends

Often when someone has a drug problem, he or she stops spending as much time with family and friends. Or the person may only spend time with friends who abuse drugs. If the person is abusing drugs alone, he or she may spend a lot of time alone, in his or her bedroom or at a place where he or she can be away from other people. One reason people withdraw from others is because they don't want people to know that they're abusing drugs. Another reason is that after a while, abusing drugs becomes more important to the drug abuser than anything—or anyone—else.

Loss of interest in activities

Another sign that someone may have a problem is if he or she no longer seems to care about things that used to interest him or her. For example, maybe the person used to love playing basketball, but suddenly doesn't want to anymore. Or maybe a person used to be involved in many after-school activities, but now goes straight home, or will only go out with a certain group of friends. As mentioned above, people who abuse drugs often become withdrawn. They don't have time to spend on other activities because they are too busy trying to get their drugs. They also realize that spending time with friends and other people who don't use drugs puts them at risk of having their drug abuse discovered.

Another common sign that someone has a drug or other problem is a loss of interest in school—for example, someone who used to spend a lot of time studying and doing homework may suddenly act as if he or she doesn't care about grades anymore. Drugs may not be the reason for this, but it is true that abusing drugs could make it hard for a person to concentrate, stay awake, or remember things. Sometimes this can lead to a downward spiral, and as the person gets more and more discouraged, he or she may take more drugs to try to "feel better" or "forget" his or her problems.

Falling grades is another possible sign of a problem. If a student with a B average suddenly starts getting Cs and Ds, this could be a sign of a problem, possibly a drug problem. Often when a person becomes a regular drug abuser, school becomes less important. Even if the abuser wants to keep getting good grades, he or she has a harder time concentrating and sometimes even staying awake. The abuser may also spend more and more time trying to get the drugs and has less time for schoolwork or any other activities.

Change in appearance

If a person goes from looking very neat and clean to sloppy, as though he or she needs a shower, this could be another sign of a drug or other problem. Often when someone is a heavy drug user, getting high becomes the main goal, and everything else seems unimportant. A change in appearance also could be due to sleep problems related to drug abuse. For example, the person might have dark eye circles or under-eye bags. Some people may also smell like medicine or chemicals.

WHAT YOUNG PEOPLE CAN DO

If you want to help stop the spread of OTC drug abuse, the first thing to do is learn as much as you can about the problem. Learn about the risks of OTC drug abuse and be able to tell them to someone who tries to tell you that it's safe to take large doses of OTC drugs. By educating yourself and then your friends, you can help prevent people you care about from putting themselves in danger.

Some students have created Web sites to help spread awareness about OTC drug abuse and its dangers. Others are working together to help pass laws to keep stores from selling certain OTC drugs to people younger than 18. You can find out what people are doing in your community by talking to your school guidance counselor or other school officials. If nothing is being done at your school, tell your school guidance counselor that you'd like to take action. Ask your friends to join you and set up a school club. Together, learn more about OTC drug abuse. You can print what you learn in a school newspaper or newsletter, or post them on your school's Web site.

In Ohio, a group of teenagers formed a drug-free alliance called Team Delta Max. They wanted to help stop alcohol and other drug abuse at their school. Together, they encouraged community leaders to meet and discuss drug problems in their community and talk about ways they could work together to help prevent drug abuse. They even launched a series of drug-free celebrations to help promote safe, drug-free environments.

The Web sites listed at the back of this book are a great resource to help you get started. You can learn about other teens who've survived OTC abuse and what they're doing to help spread the word about the dangers of abusing OTC drugs.

WHAT PARENTS CAN DO

Parents also need to learn as much as they can about the real dangers of OTC drug abuse. They should make a point to talk with their children about the risks. Studies show that young people are less likely to abuse drugs if they talk openly with their parents about drugs. According to The Partnership for a Drug-Free America (www.drugfree.org), young people whose parents tell them about the dangers of using drugs are half as likely to try or use drugs compared to teenagers whose parents do not have this kind of discussion. But although nine out of ten parents report talking to their teens about the dangers of drugs, less than one-third of teens say they've learned about these risks from their parents. The organization also reports that three out of five parents say they've talked with their kids about illicit drugs, such as marijuana, but only one-third said that they had discussed the dangers of abusing prescription and over-the-counter drugs.

Another way parents can help prevent OTC drug abuse is to teach their kids to respect all medicines. As part of teaching their kids about medicines, parents should explain how important it is that medicines are only taken for the symptoms that they are meant to treat. It is also important to point out that taking medicine when not sick is very unhealthy and dangerous. Parents should also explain the importance of taking the correct dose.

Finally, parents should learn what the signs are for OTC and other drug abuse, so that they can be alert for signs of trouble. They should also be alert for empty cough medicine bottles or packages in trash cans at home, or in their teenager's backpack or room. Finding OTC drugs in those places is a warning sign. Parents should always know what medicines are in their home, where they are stored, and how often they need to be replaced. If they seem to be running out of certain OTC drugs more frequently, that could be a cause for concern. Only medicines that are needed on a regular basis or in case of emergency should be kept in the home. Any prescription medicines that are out of date should be thrown away.

OVERDOSE: KNOW THE RISKS

An overdose happens when someone takes too much of a certain drug. Some overdoses are intentional, while others are accidental. Accidental overdoses happen when someone takes too much of a drug by mistake, or isn't aware that the amount that he or she took is too much for his or her body to handle. But some people overdose on purpose because they like the side effects, or because they want to hurt themselves. Whatever the reason, an overdose should be taken seriously. It can be deadly.

When a person overdoses from a drug, his or her body has become overwhelmed by the drug's contents and can't get rid of the drug fast enough. The bigger the amount the person took, the stronger the body's reaction will be.

SYMPTOMS OF AN OVERDOSE

There are many signs that someone is overdosing, and those signs can differ depending on what type of drug the person took. Some common signs include:

- A blue color around the lips, mouth, and nose
- Blood in vomit, urine, or feces
- Burning pain in the throat
- Burning pain in the stomach
- Double vision
- Fast, uncontrollable eye movements
- Fever
- Seizures
- Trouble breathing
- Trouble swallowing
- Vomiting

If you know someone has taken a large amount of a medication or other drug, you should call for help even if that person doesn't show symptoms. It's not always clear if someone is overdosing. The person may even just appear to be sleeping.

People who are at the greatest risk of overdosing are young people, elderly people, and people who abuse IV drugs (drugs you put in your body with a needle). Knowing what to do in case of an emergency could save lives.

WHAT TO DO IN AN EMERGENCY

If you suspect someone might have taken too much of an OTC drug, call your local poison control center at

(800) 222–1222. If the person has collapsed or stopped breathing, call 911 or your local medical emergency number and tell the person on the line exactly what is happening and where you are. Follow the person's instructions until medical help arrives.

When emergency help arrives, they will check to see if the person is breathing. They'll also check the person's heart rate, blood pressure, and temperature. They may try to get the person to vomit by giving him or her a special kind of syrup that is meant to cause vomiting. In some cases, a tube may be inserted into the person's nose, down the throat, and into the stomach. The stomach contents are sucked out through the tube, and then a saltwater mixture is injected into the tube to wash out the stomach, and then sucked out again. This is what is commonly referred to as having your stomach pumped.

The person may also be given something to make him or her go to the bathroom as a way to rid the body of the drug. If the person isn't breathing, he or she may have to go through a procedure that involves having a tube inserted through the mouth and into the trachea (windpipe) to keep the person's airway open so he or she can breathe.

An overdose patient may also have a needle inserted into the arm or back of the hand to help the body "detox." The needle is connected to a bag containing a saltwater mixture, which is dripped into the body to help flush out the drug's chemicals. This procedure can also help fix any dehydration and the body's balance of fluids and minerals.

Another procedure sometimes used involves pumping blood out of the body, filtering drugs out of the blood, and then pumping the blood back in again. This procedure may be used if the person's kidneys were damaged due to overdose. The kidneys normally do the work of filtering harmful substances out of the blood.

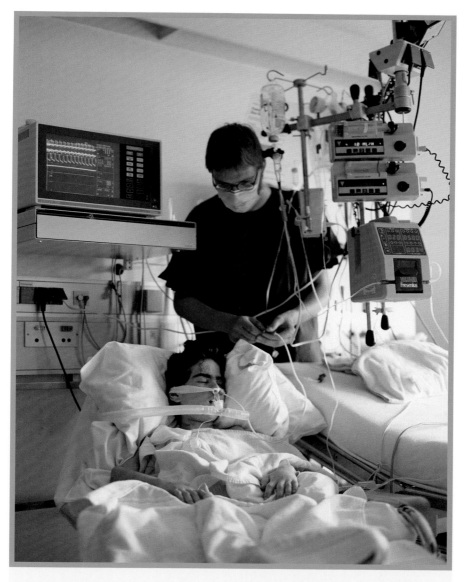

People suffering from overdoses may lose their ability to breathe prop-erly, forcing doctors or emergency medical technicians to perform an intubation. By placing a long, flexible tube down a patient's throat, medical professionals can keep the airways clear of obstructions or mucous and directly provide oxygen to the lungs. Patients must be sedated during the intubation procedure and cannot eat or drink while the tube is in place.

CALLING 911

If you make a call about someone overdosing, you may be asked to explain:

- What type of drug the person took. The person on the phone may also ask if you have the container.
- How much the person took, although it's not always possible to tell
- How long ago the person took the drug
- Whether the person took the drug with alcohol or any other drugs
- How old the person is
- What symptoms the person has
- If the person is conscious (awake, alert)
- If the person is breathing

The person may also be given another drug to balance out the one in his or her system. For example, N-acetylcysteine is a medication taken through the mouth that is known to work against the effects of acetaminophen.

THE PRICE OF OVERDOSING

Some people who recover from an overdose don't take the incident seriously. But overdosing is dangerous. In some cases, overdosing can have lasting effects, especially if a person continues to do it. For example, overdosing on acetaminophen, such as Tylenol, can cause liver damage and liver failure. In some cases, a drug overdose can cause all of a person's major organs to fail, or the person's whole system to fail. The person could also develop kidney failure, bleeding disorders, and a condition that causes swelling of the brain. If the person has enough damage, he or she could require a kidney or liver transplant. If a person who overdoses doesn't get treatment quickly enough, he or she could die.

IF YOU OR SOMEONE YOU KNOW HAS A DRUG PROBLEM . . .

If you think you have a drug problem—even if you aren't sure—seek help. Talk to a trusted friend if you are afraid to get help by yourself. You could get help from a parent, teacher, school counselor, or other trusted adult. There are also many resources listed at the back of this book. The first and most important step to recovery is admitting that you might have a problem. The next is getting help to stop. OTC and other drug abuse can be deadly. If you started abusing drugs to cope with other problems, help is available for those problems, too.

If you know someone who is abusing OTC drugs or another drug, talk to him or her about getting help. Drug abuse is dangerous. It may be hard to confront a friend, but in the long run, you'll be helping him or her. And you'll know you did all you could to help.

GLOSSARY

Addiction   A physical dependence on a substance, such as a drug, that results in the person going to extreme lengths to get and take the substance

Antihistamine   A substance that blocks the chemicals that cause cold and allergy symptoms

Antitussive   A medicine used to help stop or reduce coughing

Central nervous system   The brain and spinal cord, which work together to control the body

Codeine   A chemical made from opium or morphine (but considered safer) that is used in medicines to help stop coughing and relieve pain

Dextromethorphan (DXM)   A cough suppressant similar to codeine, but considered safer and non-addictive

Dissociative drug   A drug that causes a person to feel apart from his or her body (commonly referred to as out-of-body experiences or hallucinations)

Distributed   Given out or sold

Drug facts label   The label on all over-the-counter drugs that lists the chemical ingredients, recommended doses, and warnings for that drug

Ecstasy   A synthetic (man-made) drug that makes moods more intense and can cause hallucinations

Ephedrine   Dangerous ingredient once found in OTC diet pills

Expectorant   A type of medicine used to help the body cough up mucus or phlegm

Guaifenesin   A type of expectorant

Hallucinate   To see visions or images that do not exist

Histamine   A chemical released by the body during an allergic reaction

Illicit   Illegal

Intoxicated   Under the influence of alcohol or other drugs

Manufactured   To make or process a raw material into a finished product

Marijuana   The dried flowers and leaves of a cannabis plant that when smoked or eaten can produce a high feeling

Narcolepsy   A disorder that causes unexpected periods of deep sleep

OTC   Stands for "over the counter"

Phenylpropanolamine   A dangerous drug once used in some OTC diet pills

Prescription   A written order or direction from a doctor for taking medication or using a medical device, such as eye-glasses

Self-esteem   How a person feels about him- or herself

Side effect   The unintended mental or physical reactions to a medication or therapy

Suppressant   A type of cough medicine that works by tricking the brain into telling the body that it does not need to cough

Withdrawal   The process of stopping drug use. Symptoms of withdrawal may include nausea, vomiting, body shakes, and sleep problems.

BIBLIOGRAPHY

Blane, Jason. "Over-the-Counter Drug Abuse." *Teen People Magazine*, March 2004.

"Cough and Cold Medicine Abuse." The Nemours Foundation, February 2004. Available online. URL: www.kidshealth.org/parent/positive/talk/cough_cold_medicine_abuse.html. Accessed October 12, 2007.

"Cough Medicine Abuse by Kids." CBS News, December 29, 2003. Available online. URL: www.cbsnews.com/stories/2003/12/29/health/main590535.shtml. Accessed October 12, 2007.

"Cough Medicine Abuse by Teens." Staywell Solutions, 2007. Available online. URL: http://carefirst.staywellsolutionsonline.com/RelatedItems/1,2617. Accessed October 12, 2007.

"Dextromethorphan (DXM)." Streetdrugs.org, December 20, 2006. Available online. URL: www.streetdrugs.org/dxm.htm. Accessed October 12, 2007.

Di Laoura Devore, Cynthia. *Kids in Crisis: Kids & Drugs*. Minneapolis, Minn.: Abdo Consulting Group, 1994.

Donaldson James, Susan. "Robotripping Grows in 9–17 Age Group." ABC News, December 5, 2006. Available online. URL: http://abcnews.go.com/Health/story?id=2702166&page=1. Accessed October 12, 2007.

"A Dose of Prevention." Community Anti-Drug Coalitions of America, August 27, 2007. Available online. URL: www.doseofprevention.com. Accessed October 12, 2007.

"Drug Overdose." EMedicineHealth, August 10, 2005. Available online. URL: http://www.emedicinehealth.com/drug_overdose/article_em.htm. Accessed October 12, 2007.

"Drug Overdose." Gale Encyclopedia of Medicine, August 14, 2006. Available online. URL: www.healthatoz.com/healthatoz/Atoz/common/standard/transform.jsp?requestURI=/healthatoz/Atoz/ency/drug_overdose.jsp. Accessed September 19, 2007.

"DXM (Dextromethorphan)." Greater Dallas Council on Alcohol and Drug Abuse, July 12, 2005. Available online. URL: www.gdcada.org/statistics/dxm.htm. Accessed October 12, 2007.

"Energy Drinks: Power Boosts or Empty Boasts?" Substance Abuse and Mental Health Services Administration, April 30, 2007. Available online. URL: www.family.samhsa.gov/monitor/energydrinks.aspx. Accessed September 18, 2007.

"Fact Sheet: Prescription and Over-the-Counter Drug Abuse." Connecticut Clearinghouse and the National Clearinghouse for Alcohol and Drug Information, 2000. Available online. URL: www.ctclearinghouse.org. Accessed October 16, 2007.

"FAQs About Dextromethorphan." Consumer Healthcare Products Association, June 2007. Available online. URL: www.chpa-info.org/ChpaPortal/PressRoom/FAQs/Dextromethorphan.htm. Accessed July 11, 2007.

"FDA: The Nation's Premier Consumer Protection and Health Agency." U.S. Food and Drug Administration (brochure), January 2002.

"Generation RX: National Study Confirms Abuse of Prescription and Over-The-Counter Drugs." The Partnership for a Drug-Free America, September 21, 2006. Available online. URL: www.drugfree.org/OffsiteLinks/PATS1. Accessed October 16, 2007.

Homeier. Barbara P. "Caffeine." The Nemours Foundation, September 2004. Available online. URL: www.kidshealth.org/teen/drug_alcohol/drugs/caffeine.html. Accessed October 16, 2007.

"Increasing Number of California Teens Abuse Over-the-Counter Cold Medicine." *Pediatrics & Adolescent Medicine*, December 4, 2006.

Kaplan, Karen, and Seema Mehta. "Teens Try Cough Medicine for a High." *LA Times*, December 5, 2006.

Kittinger, Paul, and Devon Herrick. "Patient Power: Over-the-Counter Drugs." Publication no. 524, National Center for Policy Analysis, August 22, 2005.

Klosterman, Lorrie. *The Facts About Over-the-Counter Drugs.* New York: Marshall Cavendish, 2007.

"Learn About Cough Medicine Abuse (Five Moms: Stopping Teen Cough Medicine Abuse)." Consumer Healthcare Products Association, 2007. Available online. URL: www.fivemoms.com/?page_id=30. Accessed October 16, 2007.

"Legal but Lethal: The Danger of Abusing Over-the-Counter Drugs." United States Department of Health and Human Services, May 11, 2006. Available online. URL: http://family.samhsa.gov/get/otcdrugs.aspx. Accessed October 16, 2007.

Louden, Kathleen. "Over-the-Counter Drug Abuse." *Nursing Spectrum*, February 27, 2006.

"Make Up Your Own Mind About Cough Medicine Abuse." The Partnership for a Drug-Free America, November 15, 2006. Available online. URL: www.dxmstories.com. Accessed October 16, 2007.

McCutcheon, Chuck. "Abuse of Cold Remedy Spreading Quickly: Drug Industry Works to Limit Access to DXM." *Newhouse News Service*, April 18, 2004.

The MedMaster Patient Drug Information Database, a service of the U.S. National Library of Medicine and the National Institutes of Health, January 2007. Available online. URL: www.nlm.nih.gov/medlineplus. Accessed October 16, 2007.

Mogil, Cindy R. *Swallowing a Bitter Pill: How Prescription and Over-the-Counter Drug Abuse is Ruining Lives—My Story.* Far Hills, N.J.: New Horizon Press, 2001.

"New Danger in Weight-Loss Pills." Health A to Z, June 2007. Available online. URL: www.healthatoz.com/healthatoz/Atoz/common/standard/transform.jsp?requestURI=/healthatoz/Atoz/hl/nutr/vita/alert10302000.jsp. Accessed September 17, 2007.

"The New Drug Facts Label." National Council on Patient Information and Education, November 17, 2007. Available online. URL: http://www.bemedwise.org/label/label.htm. Accessed September 17, 2007.

"Non Prescription Products." U.S. Food and Drug Administration, Center for Drug Evaluation and Research, June 7, 2006. Available online. URL: www.fda.gov/cder/Offices/OTC/default.htm. Accessed October 16, 2007.

"Ohio Youth Take Drug-Free Message to Statehouse." Drug-Free Action Alliance, October 23, 2007. Available Online. URL: www.drugfreeactionalliance.org/docs/rruadannWEB_001.pdf. Accessed November 27, 2007.

"Over-the-Counter Drug Abuse." Teen Drug Abuse. Available online. URL: www.teendrugabuse.us/over_the_counter_drug_abuse.html. Accessed October 16, 2007.

"Overdose Interventions." Publication: SB 1695 Implementation. California Department of Alcohol and Drug Programs, 2003.

"Preventing Teen Cough Medicine Abuse: A Parent's Guide." Publication no. JP5–06/250M. Consumer Healthcare Products Association, 2006.

"The Progression of Liver Disease." American Liver Foundation, February 20, 2007. Available online. URL: www.liverfoundation.org/education/info/progression. Accessed October 16, 2007.

Reed, Diane. "Parents Rally in Wake of Student's Death." *Anaheim Hills News*, November 28, 2006.

Sanberg, Paul, and Richard M.T. Krema. *Over-the-Counter-Drugs: Harmless or Hazardous?* New York: Chelsea House Publishers, 1986.

Strindberg, Amanda, and Heather Ignatin. "Growing Drug Abuse Threat: Over-the-Counter Medication." *The Orange County News*, May 18, 2006.

"Study: Teens Getting High on Legal Drugs." CNN, December 21, 2006. Available online. URL: www.cnn.com/

2006/HEALTH/12/21/drug.survey. Accessed October 16, 2007.

"Teens and Prescription Drugs." *The Washington Times,* August 14, 2007.

Thompson, Colleen. "Dangerous Methods of Weight Control." Mirror-Mirror, July 27, 2007. Available online. URL: www.mirror-mirror.org/dangerou.htm. Accessed September 17, 2007.

"The Truth on Laxatives, etc." HealthyPlace.com, 2000. Available online. URL: www.healthypace.com/Communities/Eating_Disorders/peacelovehope/laxatives.asp. Accessed September 17, 2007.

"Tylenol May Cause Serious Liver Damage." *Anesthetics News,* July 5, 2006.

"What Every Parent Needs to Know about Cough Medicine Abuse." The Partnership for a Drug-Free America, October 16, 2006. Available online. URL: www.drugfree.org/Parent/Resources/Cough_Medicine_Abuse. Accessed April 30, 2007.

FURTHER READING

BOOKS

Bird, Stephen, B., Joan McClure, and Steven L. Jaffe. *Pain Relievers, Diet Pills, & Other Over-The-Counter Drugs.* New York: Chelsea House, 2000.

Hyde, Margaret O., and John F. Setaro. *Drugs 101.* Minneapolis, Minn.: 21st Century, 2003.

Karson, Jill, ed. *Teen Addiction.* Chicago: Greenhaven Press, 2006.

Klosterman, Lorrie. *The Facts About Over-the-Counter Drugs.* New York: Marshall Cavendish, 2007.

Kuhn, Cynthia, Scott Swartzwelder, and Wilkie Wilson. *Just Say Know: Talking with Kids about Drugs and Alcohol.* New York: W.W. Norton and Company, 2002.

Lawton, Sandra Augustyn, ed. *Drug Information for Teens: Health Tips About the Physical and Mental Effects of Substance Abuse.* 2nd ed. Detroit, Mich.: Omnigraphics, 2006.

Packer, Alex J., Pamela Espeland Packer (ed.), and Jeff Tolbert (Ill.) *Highs! Over 150 Ways to Feel Really, Really Good . . . Without Alcohol or Other Drugs.* Minneapolis, Minn.: Free Spirit Publishing, 2000.

WEB SITES

NIDA FOR TEENS: THE SCIENCE BEHIND DRUG ABUSE

http://teens.drugabuse.gov

The National Institute on Drug Abuse's Web site provides facts about drugs and features interactive learning games and quizzes. Teens talk about drugs, drug addiction, and how they got help.

JUST THINK TWICE: STREET SMART PREVENTION

http://www.justthinktwice.com

This Web site, run by the U.S. Drug Enforcement Agency (DEA), provides information about cough medicine abuse,

DXM, and illegal drugs. It has interactive features, animation, and videos of teens talking about their experiences with drug abuse and peer pressure.

CHECK YOURSELF

http://checkyourself.com

This site is run by The Partnership for a Drug-Free America. It has quizzes, drug information, message boards, questions and answers, and videos of teens telling their stories about drug addiction.

MAKE UP YOUR OWN MIND ABOUT COUGH MEDICINE

www.dxmstories.com

This site shows animated cartoons about the effects of cough medicine abuse. It also has video clips of young people who have been addicted to DXM. The site is run by The Partnership for a Drug-Free America.

PHOTO CREDITS

INDEX

ABOUT THE AUTHORS

JOHANNA KNOWLES has been writing nonfiction for children, teens, and adults for more than 10 years. She has published numerous pamphlets and booklets about health and social issues for young people. Knowles has a master's degree in children's literature and teaches writing for children at the Center for the Study of Children's Literature at Simmons College. She lives in Vermont with her husband and son.

Series introduction author **RONALD J. BROGAN** is the Bureau Chief for the New York City office of D.A.R.E. (Drug Abuse Resistance Education) America, where he trains and coordinates more than 100 New York City police officers in program-related activities. He also serves as a D.A.R.E. regional director for Oregon, Connecticut, Massachusetts, Maine, New Hampshire, New York, Rhode Island, and Vermont. In 1997, Brogan retired from the U.S. Drug Enforcement Administration (DEA), where he served as a special agent for 26 years. He holds bachelor's and master's degrees in criminal justice from the City University of New York.